D0548768

July, 2001... Continuing my own journey, with my own Sarah York accompanying me in my heart — Thank you, Mom, for being the role model for curiousity.

Other Books by Sarah York

Remembering Well: Rituals for Celebrating Life and Mourning Death

Into the Wilderness

Pilgrim Heart

Pilgrim Heart

The Inner Journey Home

Sarah York

Jossey-Bass, 350 Sansome Street, San Francisco, CA 94104. Jossey-Bass is a registered trademark of Jossey-Bass Inc., A Wiley Company.

Credits on page 183.

Printed in the United States of America.
Book design by Suzanne Albertson.

Library of Congress Cataloging-in-Publication Data

York, Sarah, date.
Pilgrim heart: the inner journey home / Sarah York.—1st ed.
p. cm.
Includes bibliographical references.
ISBN 0–7879–5695–3 (alk. paper)
1. Spiritual life. 2. Pilgrims and pilgrimages. 3. York, Sarah, date. I. Title.
BL624 .Y67 2001
248.4—dc21 01-00061

FIRST EDITION
HB Printing 10 9 8 7 6 5 4 3 2 1

CONTENTS

For Brett, Tom, Amy, and Brad

And the world cannot be discovered by a journey of miles, no matter how long, but only by a spiritual journey, a journey of one inch, very arduous and humbling and joyful, by which we arrive at the ground at our feet, and learn to be at home.

—Wendell Berry

GRATITUDES

Writing this book was its own pilgrimage—a journey of memory and imagination that deepened my appreciation for those who reside in the home of my pilgrim heart and give me the courage to take risks and explore unknown territories.

First among those who have been companions for this journey have been the team of publishing pilgrims in the Religion in

Practice series at Jossey-Bass, particularly Sheryl Fullerton, my editor, who has supported this project while applying her literary acumen, spiritual depth, and personal wisdom in order to help me hone my prose. Mark Kerr's enthusiasm and vision have been an inspiration, and Joanne Clapp Fullagar is a miracle worker when it comes to production coordination. Also among the many wonderful people I have worked with on the Jossey-Bass team are Chandrika Madhavan, Robert Heckman, and Adrienne Biggs. Bruce Emmer, the copyeditor; Sheri Gilbert, the permissions editor; and Kelly Hughes, the publicist, have also given great gifts. This is my second book with Jossey-Bass, and again I have partnered with people whose mission is nothing less than to offer more love, justice, and hope into the world. It is a pleasure and a privilege to work with them.

Barbara Moulton offered her encouragement and helped me launch this book. Others who have been generous with feedback from their hearts, minds, and spiritual perspectives were my readers, Jerry Caris Godard, Ann Lewis, Lee Blue, Janet Harvey, Ginny Callaway, and Marcia Meier. This book is better because they widened my writing path and kept me on it.

No pilgrim should venture into wilderness (literal or metaphorical) without a guide, and I am grateful to more guides than I can name in this space. Among those who gave me a foundation for thinking about pilgrimage in the context of comparative religions were Diana Eck, H. Richard Niebuhr, and William A. Graham Jr., professors at Harvard. Sharon Daloz Parks and Vivienne Hull were superb guides during the pilgrimage I took to Iona, Scotland. Throughout this book, I have recalled material from lectures offered by each of these individuals. Roy Oswald was my guide for a pilgrimage in Thailand and Nepal, and his wife, Carol Rousch, helped prepare my heart for that incredible and life-changing journey. To them and to the other eleven pilgrims in my group, I am grateful.

Several of my pilgrim companions or other acquaintances have shared their personal stories for this book, and I thank each of them. I have created fictitious first names for some of them. Those who are named in the book are Maureen Killoran, Laurey Masterton, Lu Anne Patrick, and Jerry Engelhardt. Others who are described in these pages are either composite portraits or fully assured of their privacy and anonymity.

My beloved husband, Chuck, who has been the heart of my home for over thirty years, was the first to read my chapters. He helped me clean them up so they would be presentable enough to go out of the house.

I sometimes tell people that I have not had children of my own, but I have been a parent to my stepsons, Brett and Tom, and to my niece, Amy, each of whom lived with Chuck and me in their teens. The fact is that none of us have children of "our own." We do,

however, seek to give our children a home, both in our hearts and in the spaces we make for their learning and growing. We know that they will leave the home we make for them in order to make their own home, and we bless them as they go, hoping that the home we have given them will always be there in their pilgrim hearts. Tom died in 1998, but Chuck and I continue to feel blessed by his brief life and his dear spirit. I dedicate this book to Brett, Tom, and Amy, and to my nephew Brad, with blessings for them all.

February 2001
Fairview, North Carolina

SARAH YORK

FOREWORD

W*hen I received the very moving manuscript for* Pilgrim Heart, I was living in Ireland. I'm there now, as I write, and so this pilgrimage of mine isn't over. Two years ago I convinced my family that it would be good for all of us to spend a year in a land we had visited several times and had grown to love. When we got here, the children adapted to their new schools and my wife quickly became active and attached. But I

immediately fell into a long, mild swoon of depression. It was entirely unexpected, and it lasted more than three months.

I've already learned several lessons about this kind of pilgrimage. First, your reason for leaving home may be nothing more than the impetus to get going. When you get to your destination, you may discover that the unintended reason and the fateful fantasies that began the whole process have little to do with planning and expectation. Something else sets the odyssey in motion, and your task is to find out what the deeper story is.

I also learned that leaving home isn't as easy as I thought it would be. I discovered from a distance what my attachments there really are and who and what sustains me. Much of this had been unconscious, and gradually, in Ireland, I learned a great deal about my life in the United States. As many people confess, my body arrived in Ireland overnight, but my soul took three months to make the journey.

I have written about depression, most of my thoughts based on my experience as a therapist dealing with the dark moods of others. Friends in Ireland, knowing my philosophy of remaining faithful to the sad and empty feelings, joked with me, telling me I should "go with my depression." I did that, to the discomfort of my family, but after a month I began to sense it lifting, very slowly, like a heavy plane traveling a seemingly endless distance on a long runway.

A month after arriving in Ireland I turned sixty. Maybe this was part of the depression, too. I feel sad leaving my youth behind, and each decade pushes me further into an old age that feels foreign to someone who has always had difficulty growing up. But I don't think the sadness of aging is connected to the journey only by the coincidence of time. As Sarah York says in many different ways, our external journeys participate in an internal pilgrimage. As I imagine it, all travel, inward and outward, is soul travel. My being in Ireland is entangled with my growing older.

In my early twenties I lived in Ireland for two years as a student and member of a religious order. Being here now is a homecoming that I feel strongly. Another paradox then: leaving home was a coming home, and being in this new, old cherished home, I long for my home in New Hampshire. I can only conclude that I am always home and not home, always on pilgrimage, and always in various stages of homecoming.

I often wondered if the homelessness of people living on the streets and moving from place to place, as is the custom especially in America, is due to a deeper call to enter the home/pilgrimage story. It's a confusing tale in which to find yourself, but the alternative is worse: floating above the tension and therefore being without place.

If I could have any influence in government, I would do everything possible to help all citizens find suitable homes—not affluent

or fancy, but more than adequate as comfort for body and soul. I would also make travel inexpensive and accessible, because we also need to travel in order to discover home. I'm a strong advocate of trains and good houses.

Sarah York's manuscript arrived, then, at a good time for me. I read every word eagerly and appreciatively. It's a wise and honest book, in style simple and in substance complex—just what I prefer. It's full of heart, and so its title is appropriate, and yet its intelligence, so smooth and understated, raises it above most books on similar themes.

This book is a journey. I suggest you read it as if you're just embarking on a trip to a foreign land—with an open heart and an uncluttered mind. Then I recommend taking a journey, if only to the other side of town, but to a place of special meaning and importance. As Sarah York says, not all journeys are pilgrimages. Like her and me, you may not be inclined to keep a journal, but you can take time to reflect and talk about your experiences. This trip, great or small, will be a microcosm, a picture of your life. It will be a holy act, even if the goal of your journey is a circus or a beach. In the language I tend to use, it will be a way of caring for your soul. It will be full of mysteries, even if on the surface it appears to be only ordinary. Learn from this book how to carry out such a journey with imagination, memory, and deep attention.

February 2001 THOMAS MOORE

Pilgrim Heart

INTRODUCTION

Leaving Home, Coming Home, Finding Home

Unlike mere travel, a pilgrimage is a journey into the landscape of the soul.

—Vivienne Hull

"Are we there yet?" It was my granddaughter, Jennafer, asking this question for the umpteenth time on a day of travel that was only two hours under way. For a young child riding in an automobile, there is only one reason to take a trip: to get to a destination.

For many adults as well, travel is oriented toward reaching a destination. Pilgrimage, however, invites you to travel with your heart, guided toward an inner goal that may be as much in the journey as in the arrival. Different from an ordinary trip, pilgrimage does not even require that you have a destination. Pilgrim time is not clock time, and pilgrim space is not map space. And the answer to the question "Are we there yet?" is always yes, for "there" is *here* and "yet" is *now.*

One way to distinguish a pilgrim adventure from ordinary travel is to think about attending a reunion—college, armed services, or some other group with which you have been associated. Perhaps the most universal experience is that of returning "home" for a high school class reunion.

If you have attended a high school reunion, why did you go? Were you curious to see who had gotten gray and who had gained weight and how many in the class were still married and whether or not the person voted most likely to succeed really did do well? Did you want to show off your spouse or your children or prove to the popular kids that being a geek turned out to be very lucrative? Or did you want something more—to journey into your past and take some time to think about who you were, how others perceived you, how you have changed? Did you wish to journey back ten, twenty, thirty, forty years or more and assess what has transpired in your life during that time? Did you perhaps even want to trick time a bit and recapture some moments from your youth?

If you went back just to catch up and see some old friends, your journey was a trip. If your travel into the past was also an attempt to discover something of yourself and take a good swat at time, it had some elements of pilgrimage.

Spiritual journey takes us to the sacred sites of our past, of our world, and of our imagination. Sometimes we travel from home on pilgrimage, but our real journey is the one we take within ourselves.

In 1998, I went on two pilgrim journeys as part of a sabbatical plan. One was to the Buddhist and Hindu lands of Thailand and Nepal; the other was to the island of Iona, Scotland, ancient site of Celtic traditions both pagan and Christian. Either of these might have been an interesting vacation trip. But vacations these were not: they were pilgrimages. This book has evolved partly in response to those soul adventures, where my travels stirred reflections on what it means to leave home in order to find home, to go "there" to find "here," and to listen, always, to the voice inside saying, "Pay attention to *now.*"

> *In my case Pilgrim's Progress consisted in my having to climb down a thousand ladders until I could reach out my hand to the little clod of earth that I am.*
>
> —Carl Jung

Each chapter of this book explores the spiritual dimensions of the human quest for a sense of belonging. Because pilgrimage offers a metaphor for spiritual journey in many religious traditions, it provides a context for investigating the human longing to feel at home, not just in a house or a town or a neighborhood but in the universe, in nature, in community, and in mortal bodies—in short, in our human selves.

To Be Touched by Something Holy: Declaring Your Intent

If you want to travel with a pilgrim heart, you need to prepare for your journey. Your leave-taking for any journey may include preparatory tasks. You stop the newspaper, arrange for someone to take care of animals or children. You pay your bills and clean out the refrigerator.

If your journey is a pilgrimage, however, it will also begin with your taking some time to reflect on what you want from it. You might purchase a journal or a sketchpad and begin educating yourself about where you are going. If you pray or meditate, you use this time of spiritual reflection to open yourself to being touched by something holy.

In addition, you might set aside time to speak with others of what you want to receive from this time that you call pilgrim time.

You create an occasion to say good-bye to those who will not go with you, you declare how you want your life to change, and you offer up your fears into the open air, including your fears of the changes that may happen in your life or the lives of those you love. You acknowledge your surrender to the Spirit, which will lead you into unpredictable adventures of the soul.

By declaring your intentions or goals, you do not predict what will happen; you say why you are going. Adventure, learning, cultural enrichment, personal growth, spiritual deepening—any of these may be part of what prompts you to block out your calendar for a designated hour, day, week, or month of pilgrim time.

In 1998, when I prepared to be away for six months from the congregation I was serving at the time, I planned a service and a sermon of leave-taking, followed by a gathering where members of my congregation and I expressed our hopes and fears for this time apart. During the service, I took off my clerical robe and put on hiking boots. I came down from the pulpit and picked up my walking stick. "Today," I said, "we are going through our rituals of separation. I have traded my clerical robe for boots and a trekking skirt and declare my intent to enter a time when I am open to change and spiritual growth. I am letting go of my ministerial role—a role I have had for sixteen years—and I embark on an adventure with many unknowns. I don't really know what to expect from this time, but I do know that by separating myself

from the securities of family, community, home, and routine, I will get to know myself better and deepen my own spiritual life. I am doing something that is a little out of character for me. You see, I like my own bed and my own pillow and clean water and toilets that have seats and flush.

"But this is a pilgrimage that calls me into something like the wilderness, where I will encounter hardships but will also have some peak experiences, where I will encounter what I do not like of myself in order to be more loving with myself. I am going on this pilgrimage because I want to be more awake—more present and fully engaged with life—when I travel at home."

Preparing your heart for a time apart and declaring your intentions are just as important for less distant pilgrim journeys. If, in fact, you go on pilgrimage only a few blocks from your home (like Henry David Thoreau in his excursion to Walden Pond), it will be your time of preparation that will make your pilgrimage a journey, even without the element of travel. Your expression of intent will declare your time as *sacred* time and your space as *sacred* space.

The declaration of intent is not a trivial thing. With it, the pilgrim is saying, "I want to touch and be touched by something holy. After this experience, my life will be different. I will be different. Because I have taken this pilgrimage, I will feel more connected with myself, with others, and with the holy and creative source of life." Each pilgrim's intent is personalized, but it will have these universal features.

Just as logistical rituals such as cleaning out the refrigerator and suspending delivery of mail signal an interruption in the daily routines of life at home, so also do the leave-taking rituals of pilgrimage—rituals of dedication and purification—clear your mind and spirit of their usual clutter of worries, tensions, and routines.

Although it can be argued that you can go on a spiritual pilgrimage in your own home, I recommend leaving. As long as you are in your home, something in your space will lure you into ordinary time. The laundry piles up, e-mail messages wait to be answered, the kitchen sink is full of dishes, the lawn needs mowing, and the weeds thrive in the flowerbeds. The phone rings, and even if you don't answer it, you fret about whether it is the school calling to say that your child has just had an accident.

There is also something to be said for leaving the familiar and opening yourself to the unfamiliar. When I told my congregation of my intent for my pilgrimage to Nepal and Thailand, I did not really know what would happen. It is interesting to me to review now what I said before I left, knowing that my time away did indeed change who I was and how I was when I returned. What is important to note now is that the declaration of intent included a willingness to let go of the structures in my life and be receptive to change. It also included an awareness that while I was away, everything and

everyone I left behind would not freeze in time and space; they too would change and grow. Pilgrimage is a journey of risk and promise, and one of the risks of leaving home is that home may not be the same when you return. Perhaps that phone call you missed *was* the school; perhaps the meeting you missed at work was the one where an important decision was made; perhaps, perhaps, perhaps.

The Stages of a Pilgrimage

Your statement of intent and leave-taking rituals that allow you to declare your hopes and fears are part of the first stage of pilgrimage, *separation*. Pilgrimage is not just about leaving ordinary life. It is much more—a process that involves stages of moving from ordinary space into sacred space and then back into ordinary space, from structure to nonstructure and then back to structure. The stages of pilgrimage—as of any life transition—are important, even to those who do not travel any distance, because they are more about what occurs within the pilgrim than about the physical process of leaving and returning home.

Pilgrimage is a journey of risk and promise, and one of the risks of leaving home is that home may not be the same when you return.

In the first stage, *separation,* the pilgrim leaves the familiar for the strange, leaves the known for the unknown. Leaving home is a common theme in the archetypal stories from many religious traditions. Buddha left home entirely, never to return; Jesus called his disciples to leave everything and follow him; Jewish slaves were freed from bondage in Egypt, but they left their home behind and entered the wilderness. Muhammad fled to the dessert, where he received his revelations from Allah and wrote the Koran. Modeled on these archetypal journeys, pilgrimage calls for a letting go of the structures of life that are commonly thought of as "home." Contemporary pilgrimage, however, follows a more circular path, where one leaves in order to return more spiritually aware, rather than abandoning family to seek the spiritual life.

During the stage of separation, pilgrims may practice rituals of cleansing or purification. Muslims who embark on the *hajj,* their pilgrimage to Mecca, put on a white garment and perform ablutions; Hindus who travel to Banaras, India's holy city on the Ganges River, similarly perform rites of cleansing. Before they set out on their pilgrim journey to Wirikuta, the mythical home of their ancestors, Huichol Indians of Mexico have what is called a "knotting-in" ceremony. Their guide literally binds them together to symbolize their affection and trust as a group. Then they all confess their illicit sexual exploits and are cleansed.

In the first stage of pilgrimage, you prepare to cross a threshold from the known to the unknown, and your rituals of cleansing or confession voice your openness to being touched and changed

by a power that is holy and transcendent. When a group is beginning a pilgrimage together, this is a time for the group to form the bonds of spiritual kinship.

My sabbatical journey to Nepal and Thailand was a pilgrim adventure with eleven other men and women from the United States. Our guides, Roy Oswald and Carol Rousch, did their own version of a knotting-in ceremony. Our group gathered on the eve of our journey for some rituals of bonding, including the usual "getting to know you" activities, complete with confessing our Myers-Briggs personality types. We had already identified the introverts as the ones who wanted to have their own private tents and the extroverts as the ones who needed to tell us about every prescription drug they had in their possession for the treatment of diarrhea. Then there was the matter of whether we were more perceiving (P) or more judging (J). The Ps were the ones who had packed the night before and had already misplaced their plane tickets. The Js, by contrast, had separate little sacks for socks and underwear and a collapsible or expandable suitcase for packing purchases. I was sort of a J/P: I had six different places to hide my money, but I forgot where they were. Although we joked

You prepare to cross a threshold from the known to the unknown, and your rituals of cleansing or confession voice your openness to being touched and changed by a power that is holy and transcendent.

about how the Ps and the Js might clash, there was an element of self-revelation and awareness of our differences in this exercise that would serve us well during our shared adventures.

Other rituals of bonding included making agreements with regard to how we would be together. We had all read Scott Peck's book *A Different Drum,* in which he discusses the stages of community, and it was part of our covenant that we were prepared to get past the initial stage of "pseudo-community" and deal with the chaos, conflicts, or tensions that we might encounter during our time together. Roy and Carol had been guides for several pilgrim groups, and I guess they knew there might be some tensions among us.

The next stage of pilgrimage is *crossing the threshold.* Pilgrims move from ordinary time and space into sacred time and sacred space, where things can be turned upside down. The structures that define who you are in your ordinary life become irrelevant. Pilgrim space has no regard for class, race, or economic status. A ritual of crossing over may be something as literal as walking through a doorway or over a line drawn on the ground. This is the point at which pilgrims most need a guide, for they enter a space where there is potential for danger. Stripping away the usual structures of life, however, also opens the way to possibility.

Once over the threshold, the pilgrim enters the third stage, *transformation.* This is the heart of the pilgrimage and always

involves an element of inner conflict or struggle. It is time spent in the wilderness within, where you meet your fears and confront them—where you come up against whatever prevents you from hearing the voice of the Spirit or living a life of compassion and generosity.

The difference between a pilgrim's ordeal and the conflicts one encounters in ordinary time (for example, a bout with depression, a family feud, or a struggle to make ends meet) is that it is voluntary. It is chosen. The pilgrim knows that there is no growth without inner confrontation, no promised land without time in the wilderness, no mountaintop that can be reached without going through the valley of the shadow of death.

> *The pilgrim knows that there is no growth without inner confrontation, no promised land without time in the wilderness, no mountaintop that can be reached without going through the valley of the shadow of death.*

The final stage of pilgrimage is *reincorporation*. The pilgrim leaves in order to return, and upon returning, reenters the roles or structures that were irrelevant during the pilgrimage. Since the pilgrim has been changed by the experience of battling with the demons or struggling with the elements, this may require some adjustment. You don't just return home to the same old routines and the same old ways of being. Because you are different, home is also different. Or is it? What difference does it make that you have made this inner journey? How will other people in your life be affected?

What Is a Pilgrim Heart?

Pilgrim Heart is the title I have given this book because it is not so much about pilgrimage or travel as it is about approaching life with the heart of a pilgrim.

A pilgrim heart is first of all an open heart—receptive to change and growth. The paradox of pilgrimage is that you have to leave your comfort zone in order to explore the spiritual growing edges that take you into a deeper level of comfort. You have to be willing to let go of the security of your physical home in order to open yourself to your spirit's home. Because you are away from home as a pilgrim, you have an opportunity to consider what it means to be "at home" within yourself.

The paradox of pilgrimage is that you have to leave your comfort zone in order to explore the spiritual growing edges that take you into a deeper level of comfort. You have to be willing to let go of the security of your physical home in order to open yourself to your spirit's home.

The chapters of this book follow the cyclical pattern of the pilgrim path. Chapter One explores some of the deeper stirrings of the pilgrim heart that prompt the search for a sense of home.

Chapter Two takes up the topic of facing some of the fears and struggles that arise when we venture into sacred landscape. Chapters Three and Four take the pilgrim deeper into the aspect of wilderness struggle and explore the personal and cultural obstacles we encounter as we seek to be at home in the natural world and in our bodies. Chapter Five places the individual pilgrim in the context of a larger social identity, where spiritual experience inspires visions for human community. In Chapter Six, the pilgrim returns home to ordinary space and time after having experienced this time apart from time and having been transformed by encounters with the holy and reincorporates into his or her community and environment. The goal of the journey, after all, is to become more . . . *at home.*

chapter one

Where Do You Come From?

O seekers, remember, all distances are traversed by those who yearn to be near the source of their being.

—Matthew Fox

W*e measure our lives year by year,* from birthday to birthday; from childhood to youth to adulthood to old age. But our memories do not store away years or months, or even weeks or days. They catalogue images or scenes or snatches of conversation and file them where it may take no more than the scent of a lilac to stir these fragments into consciousness. On occasions when our souls are deeply moved, our memories record only moments—timeless moments when the universe is distilled and we receive a brief glimpse of our place in it all.

I recall such a moment when I was a long way from home, on a trail high in the Himalayas, trekking through the Anapurna region of Nepal. I was separated from everyone else in our little pack of thirteen pilgrims from the United States. Walking at different paces, we would often spread out from three to five miles along the path.

At this particular time, I had just climbed up a steep and treacherous path to the top of a hill with two other women. I had a bone spur on the bottom of one foot, which means that I had to stop about every hour and a half, take off my shoes, and rest the foot for fifteen or twenty minutes. The others weren't ready to stop for that long, so they went on. I sat on a bench at the edge of a steep decline. For fifteen minutes, no one came along the path. I just sat there, sipping from my water bottle and looking out into the river valley and the mountains beyond—draped in snow, shedding their winter white into the rocky riverbed below.

In the still quiet of those moments, time stopped. I suddenly felt intensely alone, acutely aware of being in a strange and distant land. I had no thoughts, only a sense of being unconnected to anyone or anything familiar and aware of my own insignificance in that vast and magnificent setting. It was not a euphoric suspension, however. It was more like what theologians call existential angst or what Rev. Judith Walker-Riggs has called "cosmic vertigo."[1] It was as though my soul was homesick, but I did not know what it was

homesick for. I forgot where and who I was in that brief moment out of time.

I was sitting there feeling this holy restlessness when I was jingled back into the present by the familiar sound of a bell, announcing someone on horseback. Looking up, I saw a Nepali man smiling down at me from atop his horse.

"Where do you come from?" he asked.

"The United States," I said. "California."

"No, no," he said. "I mean, where do you come from *today*?"

"Oh," I said. "Tatopani."

"I come from Tatopani too. One hour." He pointed down to the horse and let out a hearty laugh. He knew that I had been about five strenuous hours on foot to his one hour on horseback. I joked with him about letting me ride the horse before he galloped off, still laughing.

I sat there high on a mountain in the Himalayas, exhausted, surrounded by immense beauty, my foot in pain. As the sound of the bell on the traveler's horse echoed down the trail, his poignant question lingered: "Where do you come from?" I sat there having a bout with cosmic vertigo . . . and I knew that having that bout was one reason I had gone so far away.

Where do you come from? How would you answer that question? When you think of home, is it the place where you live? Is it the house of your childhood or the town where you grew up? Do you even have a place that you call your hometown?

I grew up in southern California. My early childhood memories are less of a hometown and more of a house, a yard, and a home *street* within walking distance of my school, the miniature golf course, and the ice-cream stand. My sense of hometown was not the city of North Hollywood but rather an area contained within a few blocks of Cartwright Street. I remember it more in terms of events than in terms of place—neighborhood gatherings where all the men took turns churning the homemade ice cream; warm summer evenings putt-putting through the miniature golf village; Brownie meetings at the Morrows'; Sunday dinners at the Rosenes'; camp-outs in the backyard; and bike excursions to the drugstore on Lankershim Boulevard.

When I was twelve, we moved to Florida, where I lived until I graduated from college. By that time, my parents had built a summer home in North Carolina, where they established their full-time residence after a few years.

My careers took me to several other places, any one of which might have become home for me. In my mid-twenties, I returned to California, where I met my husband, Chuck. But after getting shaken up by an earthquake and encountering sticker shock when we wanted to buy a house, we moved to North Carolina. From there we went to Boston, Long Island, and suburban Maryland. In

every place we lived, we hung pictures, planted flowers, and established a first-name relationship at a favorite Chinese restaurant. We called it home, enjoying connections in the community and appreciating the beauty of the natural settings.

Somehow, however, we knew we were not truly home. We knew that our souls were called to be in another place and that eventually we would find our way there. Perhaps that place was in western North Carolina, where my parents had lived and we owned property; perhaps it was somewhere else. We did not know.

Eventually, a career opportunity took us back to southern California. Chuck's mother still lived in the same house where he had grown up, and other family members were nearby. Although my parents had died, my brother was in California, too. Each day that I drove to work, I passed the house where my parents had lived when my older brother was born. We thought we had returned home.

A few months after we moved back to California, however, I announced to Chuck, "I'm homesick."

"Yeah, me too," he said. "But I don't know what I'm homesick for."

I understood exactly what he meant. We had never felt at home in the suburbs of Washington, D.C., where we had lived for five years before the move. Chuck was not homesick for an hour's commute to work, and as much as we had liked our house in Maryland, we weren't homesick for that either. We missed our friends and the people at work, but we weren't really homesick for them. We missed them, and missing isn't the same as feeling homesick.

We were both rather stumped. Here we were with this homesick feeling, but we didn't have a particular place we were homesick for. We had come back to what should have felt like home, where Chuck's boyhood room was just a short drive away and a whiff of eucalyptus could take me back to my childhood home on Cartwright Street and the gummy-scented trees that lined the sidewalk. Perhaps it was something in the scent of the eucalyptus that prompted me to return then, for the first time in forty years, to the house on Cartwright Street.

We drove there on the Ventura Freeway, whose pavement beneath our tires had replaced the Rosenes' house and most of the block that had comprised my young world. A new street had devoured our next-door neighbors' home, converting our mid-block lot to a corner lot with a view of the steep, sloping bank next to the freeway. I smiled in secret triumph when I noticed that the new street was called Sarah Street. Where we used to have a large yard to the other side of our home, there was now another house.

The white picket fence that bordered our front yard was gone.

The eucalyptus trees were gone.

And even though the house had been spared in the routing of the freeway, it had definitely *shrunk*. The two-story mansion of memory was actually a modest little cottage.

Thomas Wolfe was right: you can't go home again.

You can't go home again because home is not what it was and you are not who you were.

You can't go home again because it has changed and you have changed.

Home, it turns out, is more in time than it is in space, more in events than in time, more in people than in events, more in our own minds than in people. Home is ours to create and to long for, to remember and to dream about.

You can't go home again because home is not what it was and you are not who you were. You can't go home again because it has changed and you have changed.

When I think about the nostalgic pilgrimages I have taken to the homes of my childhood, they evoke a sense of home that is more than the security of my parents' love and more than a neighborhood community. They evoke a state of mind that belongs only to a child. I think of Dylan Thomas's description of his childhood in the poem "Fern Hill." The poem begins:

Now as I was young and easy under the apple boughs

About the lilting house and happy as the grass was green,
  The night above the dingle starry,
    Time let me hail and climb
  Golden in the heydays of his eyes,
And honoured among wagons I was prince of the apple towns
And once below a time I lordly had the trees and leaves
    Trail with daisies and barley
Down the rivers of the windfall light.[2]

Several more stanzas evoke the world of the child, where in those "lamb white days" the sun is "born over and over" and the moon is "always rising." Then in the final stanza, Thomas offers an image that speaks to the condition of the homesick soul:

Oh as I was young and easy in the mercy of his means,
  Time held me green and dying
Though I sang in my chains like the sea.[3]

When we are young, we may have times we feel homesick. But we are homesick for a familiar place, usually a place where we know there are people who love and accept us. When we are older, we are homesick for that fern-hill feeling we had as a child, that feeling of being the prince of apple towns, the princess of orchard villages. Our nostalgia is less for what we have lost and more for

our youthful ability to live without time chafing at our carefree days with reminders that we are on a temporary visa to Planet Earth.

Our spiritual task is not to try to go back and retrieve the days when we sang in our chains, unconscious of their tightening hold on us. It is rather to sing in our chains, fully aware that we are temporary sojourners in this world. What makes this difficult is that it is our nature to avoid this awareness—to fill up our days with activities that distract us from this consciousness rather than engage us with it.

It is also our nature, once we have emerged from childhood, to harden ourselves against time's inevitable infringement on our perceptions. Most of us were insulated as young children from the awareness of those three realities that set the young Siddhartha (Buddha) on his spiritual journey: old age, sickness, and death. Then, when suffering intruded on our youthful innocence, we began to grow the shell that protects us from being wounded again.

Frederick Buechner describes his own fern-hill years in his autobiographical book *The Sacred Journey.* His youthful bliss came to an abrupt end, however, when he was ten years old and his father committed suicide. Buechner writes:

> A child takes life as it comes because he has no other way of taking it. The world had come to an end that Saturday morning, but each time we had moved to another place, I

> had seen a world come to an end, and there had always been another world to replace it. When somebody you love dies, Mark Twain said, it is like when your house burns down; it isn't for years that you realize the full extent of your loss. For me it was longer than for most, if indeed I have realized it fully even yet, and in the meanwhile the loss came to get buried so deep in me that after a time I scarcely ever took it out to look at it at all, let alone to speak of it. If ever anybody asked how my father died, I would say heart trouble. That seemed at least a version of the truth.[4]

Young Freddy protected himself with a shell of escape and denial that served to help him survive:

> To do for yourself the best that you have it in you to do—to grit your teeth and clench your fists in order to survive the world at its harshest and worst—is, by that very act, to be unable to let something be done for you and in you that is more wonderful still. The trouble with steeling yourself against the harshness of reality is that the same steel that secures your life against being destroyed secures your life also against being opened up and transformed by the holy power that life itself comes from. You can survive

> on your own. You can grow strong on your own. You can even prevail on your own. But you cannot become human on your own.[5]

What Buechner is saying is that we don't just learn to protect ourselves from pain. We protect ourselves from joy and love. The soul's quest for home is not just a nostalgic longing for the way things were before we began protecting ourselves from the "harshness of reality." No, the longing that empowers us to become more human invites us to grieve for what is lost and open ourselves to "the holy power that life itself comes from."

To embark on a pilgrimage of the soul is to declare our openness to being touched by that holy power. At some point, or several, in my life and yours—maybe with a defining event, maybe not—the fern-hill dream-time that is oblivious to time gives way to a consciousness of our place in time, of our bodies changing every second, of our fragile and precious existence on this beautiful and mysterious planet. Perhaps then, perhaps sooner, we begin yearning for that time again—whether it was real or not—when we were at home in our bodies, in the world, and in the universe. We long for that child-time when our fears were more instinctive than learned and our hearts opened freely with unconditional trust.

Feeling homesick in ways that we cannot even explain, we set off in search of something or someone in the world that is trustable. Perhaps we set off to retrieve the part of ourselves that could trust. Because we are aware of ourselves existing in the world's ordinary time and space, we set off in search of *sacred* time and *sacred* space. We may not be able to redeem the unredeemable, so our quest is to redeem something of the sense we had, once upon a time, of being in harmony with creation.

A holy restlessness is what prompts the pilgrimage of the spirit—a journey real or metaphorical that calls us away from what we have grown to think of as our home in order to discover a deeper sense of being at home with our human nature. Sometimes the call into pilgrimage is voluntary—evoked perhaps by a spiritual awareness that our lives will be enriched by the quest.

"Why do you wonder that globe-trotting does not help you, seeing that you always take yourself with you? The reason which set you wandering is ever at your heels."

—Socrates, in Seneca the Younger, "On Travel as a Cure for Discontent"

Sometimes, however, the call to pilgrimage is not of our choosing. Like Frederick Buechner, we may be thrown into it by a life event that shatters our sense of what we can trust. When something happens to shake the foundations of our faith or disrupt our sense of home—something like a move or a marital separation or a death of a family member, or a fire or an earthquake or a tornado—when something happens to disturb what we think of as home or upset the illusion of order we have

created for ourselves, it stirs our consciousness of a deeper longing for a sense of place in space and time.

Where do you come from? It was that question from a stranger on the other side of the world that roused me from an involuntary bout with cosmic vertigo. It could just as well have been the question that would trigger such a bout, for it prompted me to consider not just where I started my day or my life but where I belonged in the larger scheme of creation.

When something happens to disturb what we think of as home or upset the illusion of order we have created for ourselves, it stirs our consciousness of a deeper longing for a sense of place in space and time.

It is, after all, integral to our human condition that we ponder our place in space and time—that we question beginnings and endings. Our ponderings, however, are likely to evoke even more questions as we seek to be at home in a boundless universe.

There is an image from *The Restaurant at the End of the Universe* by Douglas Adams that captures a sense of what kind of undertaking it is to develop a sense of our home in the cosmic scheme of things. In that book, there is a punishment chamber called the Total Perspective Vortex. The Total Perspective Vortex provides its victims with a glimpse of the entire universe in all of space and all of time. In the midst of this boundless panorama is a sign that says, "YOU ARE HERE." All those who have ever entered the chamber have gone mad, which was an indication, to the inventor at least, that the last thing we humans can afford to have is a sense of perspective.[6]

Two days after I had encountered my Himalayan version of the Total Perspective Vortex, our group of trekking pilgrims camped on the edge of a wide, rocky riverbed, in the village of Larjung. To that point, we had not yet seen the highest mountains of the Anapurna range, even though we had been on the path for several days. Dalaghiri, one of the world's most colossal peaks, was in our range of sight, but a dense mist cloaked most of it. That night, however, at sunset, the clouds retreated except for a wispy veil clinging to the top of Dalaghiri. When we came out after dinner, even the wispy veil was gone, and a full moon reflected on the white-glazed mountains. I walked out into the Kali Gandaki riverbed to get a full 360-degree view of the surrounding peaks and just stood there for several minutes, taking in this moment of grandeur in the world's deepest valley, surrounded by the world's highest mountains. In that moonlit Himalayan bowl of astounding beauty, I felt much as I had before—lost, alone, and homeless. I also felt *connected* and at home.

Curiously, it was high on the mountain that I had experienced the "valley" of my own fears and down in the valley that I had the

"peak experience" of ecstatic connection. To further underscore the paradox of these two encounters, I realize that both homesick on the peak and at home in the valley, I was lost—and found—in the vastness of creation. When the man on the horse asked me, "Where do you come from?" it occurred to me that I had come this far from home in order to feel lost in strangeness; to remove the structures of home and feel, bone-deep, an inner ache for the home I could neither describe nor remember. Now, however, I knew I was not lost or alien in the infinite universe but rather immersed in it—a *part* of its immense grandeur.

This was it. This was what the mystics write about. This was union with the Spirit, the holy creative energy of the universe. This was connection with the Universal Soul and creation itself. I found myself singing an old hymn, "How Great Thou Art," at the top of my lungs. I had not sung it for at least thirty years, since I had long since abandoned its central message. But there it was. (I discovered later that I could remember every verse.) The song, the music, the spirit of the singing, were all a spontaneous response to the moment, and I sang out the first praise-filled verse so loudly that people came out of their homes to investigate the sounds echoing through the river valley:

O Lord my God, when I in awesome wonder, consider all the worlds thy hands have made,

I see the stars, I hear the rolling thunder, thy power throughout the universe displayed.

Then sings my soul, my savior God to thee,
How great thou art, how great thou art!
Then sings my soul, my savior God to thee,
How great thou art, how great thou art!

That night the temperatures dropped to –9 degrees Celsius. The floor of my little tent was wet, and I was so chilled I could not sleep. It was the most miserable night of the trek, but my soul was singing. I felt very much at home—grateful, so incredibly grateful to be in the strange and remote village of Larjung. As the poet wrote, "Time held me green and dying, but I sang in my chains like the sea."

Being lost and found in the fullness of a cosmic void was part of the feeling that grasped me both on the mountain and in the valley. The first experience created a feeling of anxiety—an empty ache wrapped in fear. The second epiphany, only two days later, was a balm, a fullness; I was embraced by something infinitely whole. The holy paradox is that these two opposing

The holy paradox is that these two opposing feelings were in fact so akin to one another. Anxiety and ecstasy, isolation and connection, despair and hope, homelessness and feeling at home: each, it seems, must flow into and combine with its opposite.

feelings were in fact so akin to one another. Anxiety and ecstasy, isolation and connection, despair and hope, homelessness and feeling at home: each, it seems, must flow into and combine with its opposite.

"Without Contraries," wrote William Blake, "is no progression."[7] This proverb applies to the spiritual quest of the twenty-first century, which is something like singing an old hymn of praise while trapped in the Total Perspective Vortex. Most of us do not look up into "the heavens" like our ancestors of long ago and talk to God as if he were sitting up on his throne just a little bit beyond our range of view. Any sense the people of old might have had of the world as home and God as the great protective Daddy in the Sky looking after the darlings of his creation has been progressively diminished ever since Copernicus announced that the earth is not the center of the universe. Thanks to the discoveries of science, we have learned a few more things about our place in the cosmic scheme of things.

Instead of looking to heaven for some comfort that all is well, we find ourselves hoping that we don't destroy the ozone layer—the only thing that prevents us from becoming charred morsels in a cosmic microwave oven. Instead of presuming that God decorated the sky with all those sparkling lights and displays them like a moving picture for our amusement, we wonder if a giant meteor will break through our atmosphere and explode our little planet-home into stardust. Instead of sending our prayers into the sky like radio waves transmitted to the heavenly palace, we send out our little voyager machines to take pictures of planets made up entirely of swirling gases; our radio telescopes tell us of a universe so large that we cannot begin to imagine what exists.

So how do we define our place? How do we figure out where we belong in all this boundless expanse of space?

And time. How do we establish our sense of place in time? Now, instead of time that began with the event of creation according to myths handed down through centuries of religious tradition, we have time that probably did not begin at all, because to speak of a beginning is to speak as if time can be contained, and what we know now is that there is no such thing as containing time. For that matter, there is probably no such thing as time. Time is such an arbitrary thing. After all, it is feasible for someone to take off into space at a speed close to the speed of light and return twenty years later to discover that thirty thousand years have elapsed on earth.

Science reminds us of our place, not just in space but also in time. The second-brightest star in the sky, for example, is seventy-five light-years away. If I look up in the sky tonight and see it blow up I am looking at an event that happened before I was born. And it gets worse. When the light from the nearest spiral galaxy left for earth, there were no humans on the planet. However we think we tell time, it does not show up on the cosmic clock.

This means that whether or not we have abandoned religion, it can no longer provide us with a secure sense of our place in this universe of uncharted space and immeasurable time.

Still, we have our human needs. We impose our own artificial order on the chaos. We *pretend* to establish ourselves in time, for example, with our myriad timepieces—clocks and watches of every description. I recall seeing an item in the American Express catalogue that epitomizes this human compunction to contain the uncontainable. The catalogue item was called the "rush-hour clock." It would hang on a knob in the shower, it would not fog up, and you could read its large black numerals and hands right through the water. The image this evokes for me is of a planet full of naked humans, showering with their unfoggable clocks—joyless misers hoarding minutes as if they could take control of time itself. Pretty soon we will have waterproof cell phones, too.

This is our human nature, this imposing of order on that which does not take orders. Our clocks and calendars help us feel more at home where we are not at home. It is a commonly held notion that if a human being is isolated with no means of knowing time—if you take away the clocks and calendars—the person will go crazy. I know this must be true, because I've seen it in the movies. Solitary prisoners always survive by notching the days into a wall. If you lose your sense of time, you lose yourself. Keeping track of time is our way of imposing order on chaos—so we don't lose ourselves to the void.

Science has shaken religion's traditional capacity to provide humans with a sense of home in space and time. Instead of displacing religion, however, it has underscored how very little we know and how very mysterious is creation. T. S. Eliot identified the inadequacy of our cycles of "idea and action" in "Choruses from the Rock":

> All our knowledge brings us nearer to our ignorance,
> All our ignorance brings us nearer to death,
> But nearness to death no nearer to God.
> Where is the Life we have lost in living?
> Where is the wisdom we have lost in knowledge?
> Where is the knowledge we have lost in information?
> The cycles of Heaven in twenty centuries
> Bring us farther from God and nearer to the Dust.[8]

Western religion has failed to provide the sense of a familiar and containable home that used to be its stock in trade, and science has failed to replace what religion can no longer provide. The human spirit, however, continues to long for home and respond to the mystery of creation with a pilgrim heart.

When I feel homesick, I receive some kind of comfort by looking up at the stars on a clear night. No matter where I am on this planet, no matter how far away from whatever I think of as home,

the parade of constellations out there is the same. And it is part of home, too. Singing in my chains takes into account that image of the void from the Total Perspective Vortex, but there is still something in my soul that longs to sing, to praise, to declare that yes, I am part of it all in some unexplainably meaningful way.

Homesickness doesn't really have much to do with any particular place or time, past or future. It is a feeling we acquire when we become conscious of the chains of time that have bound us from the day we were born. It is the emotional trigger for a spiritual quest.

Homesickness doesn't really have much to do with any particular place or time, past or future. It is a feeling we acquire when we become conscious of the chains of time that have bound us from the day we were born. It is the emotional trigger for a spiritual quest.

In *The Message in the Bottle,* Walker Percy speaks to how important it is that we listen to the promptings of the heart and soul that set us on our pilgrim path:

> Suppose a man is a castaway on an island. He is, moreover, a special sort of castaway. He has lost his memory in the shipwreck and has no recollection of where he came from or who he is. All he knows is that one day he finds himself cast up on the beach. It is a pleasant place and he soon discovers that the island is inhabited. Indeed it turns out that the islanders have a remarkable culture with highly devel-

> oped social institutions, a good university, first-class science, a flourishing industry, and art. The castaway is warmly received. Being a resourceful fellow, he makes the best of the situation, gets a job, builds a house, takes a wife, raises a family, goes to night school, and enjoys the local arts of cinema, music, and literature. He becomes, as the phrase goes, a useful member of the community.[9]

Percy likens our lives on this planet to that of the castaway. We may not be at home in the world, but we fully involve ourselves in the enterprise of creating a comfortable and meaningful life. Because we are fully engaged in living our "island" life, we often forget that we are castaways; we may even feel very much at home on the island. The fact is, however, we are not home, and our spirits have ways of reminding us of that uncomfortable fact. We occasionally feel homesick and are not sure why. We may be in the Himalayas or standing in our own kitchen when the feeling grasps us in the full and conscious present.

This homesick feeling, however, is not remedied by going "home." Percy explains:

> A castaway, everyone would agree, would do well to pay attention to . . . knowledge of the nature of the world and news of events that are relevant to his life on the island.

> Such news, the news relevant to his survival as an organism, his life as a father and husband, as a member of a culture, . . . and so on—we can call island news. Such news is relevant to the everyday life of any islander on any island at any time.
>
> Yet even so all is not well with him. Something is wrong. For with all the knowledge he achieves, all his art and philosophy, all the island news he pays attention to, something is missing. What is it? He does not know. He might say that he was homesick except that the island is his home and he has spent his life making himself at home there. He knows only that his sickness cannot be cured by island knowledge or by island news.
>
> But how does he know he is sick, let alone homesick? He may not know. He may live and die as an islander at home on his island. But if he does know, he knows for the simple reason that in his heart of hearts he can never forget who he is: that he is a stranger, a castaway, who despite a lifetime of striving to be at home on the island is as homeless now as he was the first day he found himself cast up on the beach.[10]

Percy does not suggest any solutions for the castaway. He emphasizes, however, that we who are spiritually homeless should not pretend that we are not. Neither should we disengage with our island life in relentless pursuit of news from across the seas and ignore the home that we have made for ourselves. We should search nevertheless and live in hope that the tides will deliver the bottle with a message in it. We should hope that a message will come and that when it does, it will not be a piece of knowledge or a piece of island news. It will be news from across the cosmic seas.

Where do you come from? What are you homesick for?

Whatever it is that we call a spiritual quest, it begins with our search for news from across the seas. It begins with a holy restlessness, a sense that we cannot go home again because whatever we recall of home may be as much the home we cannot remember as it is the one we do remember.

It begins with a holy restlessness, a sense that we cannot go home again because whatever we recall of home may be as much the home we cannot remember as it is the one we do remember.

We are like castaways on an island. We don't know where we came from; we don't know what happens after we die, but we do what we can to feel at home, because we do not want to lose our minds in the Total Perspective Vortex.

What is home? What are you looking for on your quest for home?

You are looking for a place where you belong. It may be an illusion. But you are looking for it anyway.

And you are looking for a place that feels safe and peaceful—safe from evil, safe from violence, safe from anxiety, safe from loneliness; no conflict, no division, no dissension. As I said, it may be an illusion.

If you've ever had the experience of having your house robbed, you know what a creepy feeling it gives you. In my case, I felt that my home—my safe home—had been invaded by strangers. In fact, if I had been there and had been armed, it's possible I might have killed the intruders. Killed them. Me, the nonviolent pacifist. People do that, not because their property means so much to them, but because they cannot abide having the safety of their home—and their selves—threatened.

Home is sanctuary.

Home is also the feeling of acceptance. As Robert Frost put it, "Home is the place where, when you have to go there, they have to take you in. . . . Something you somehow haven't to deserve."[11]

No wonder there's no place like home. Home isn't even much like home most of the time.

The quest for home is the need to feel that we belong.

The quest for home is the need to feel safe.

The quest for home is the need to be accepted.

People who join faith communities—a spiritual home—bring all of these needs into their quest for spiritual growth. In many faith communities, weekly gatherings take place in a space that is called a "sanctuary." Literally, *sanctuary* is a sacred place, but even more than that, it is a place where we feel safe.

Cast adrift on the great sea of limitless time and space, we look to spiritual communities for mooring. Those communities offer a kind of home to their members, who gather for potluck dinners, visit one another in hospitals, and join to celebrate or observe rites of passage.

That isn't really why most of us look for a spiritual home, however. We are drawn to a spiritual home because we are homeless. We are castaways, and we know we are castaways, and we are looking for news from across the sea. We still live our island life, but we know that to be a castaway on this remote little planet means to search for our spirit's home.

The pilgrim soul's journey home begins with a decision to embark on the search.

chapter two

Leaving Home

A longing pure and not to be described
drove me to wander over woods and fields
and in a mist of hot abundant tears
I felt a world arise and live for me.

—Johann Wolfgang von Goethe, *Faust*

Parker Palmer, in *The Active Life: A Spirituality of Work, Creativity, and Caring,* describes an experience he had when he took the outdoor challenge program, Outward Bound. He calls it a parable:

> I took the course in my early forties . . . and in the middle of that course I was asked to confront the thing I had feared most since I had first heard about Outward Bound: A gossamer strand was hooked to a harness around my body, I was backed up to the top of a 110-foot cliff, and I was told

to lean out over God's own emptiness and walk down the face of that cliff to the ground eleven stories below.

I remember the cliff too well. It started with a five-foot drop to a small ledge, then a ten-foot drop to another ledge, then a third and final drop all the way down. I tried to negotiate the first drop; my feet instantly went out from under me and I fell heavily to the first ledge. "I don't think you quite have it yet," the instructor observed astutely. "You are leaning too close to the rock face. You need to lean much farther back so your feet will grip the wall."

That advice, like the advice of some spiritual traditions, went against my every instinct. Surely one should hug the wall, not lean out over the void! But on the second drop I tried to lean back; better, but not far enough, and I hit the second ledge with a thud not unlike the first. "You still don't have it," said the ever-observant instructor. "Try again."

Since my next try would be the last one, her counsel was not especially comforting. But try I did, and much to my amazement I found myself moving slowly down the rock wall. Step-by-step I made my way with growing confidence until, about halfway down, I suddenly realized that I was heading toward a very large hole in the rock, and—

not knowing anything better to do—I froze. The instructor waited a small eternity for me to thaw out, and when she realized that I was showing no signs of life she yelled up, "Is anything wrong, Parker?" as if she needed to ask. To this day I do not know the source of the childlike voice that came up from within me, but my response is a matter of public record: "I don't want to talk about it."

The instructor yelled back, "Then I think it's time you learned the Outward Bound motto." Wonderful, I thought. I am about to die, and she is feeding me bromides. But then she spoke words I have never forgotten, words so true that they empowered me to negotiate the rest of that cliff without incident: "If you can't get out of it, get into it." Bone-deep I knew that there was no way out of the situation except to go deeper into it, and with that knowledge my feet began to move.[1]

I wonder, sometimes, what it is in the human animal that sets it off on adventures like Outward Bound or on pilgrimages to strange and distant lands. Why leave the comforts of your home, for example, to camp out in the cold? Why take time from your life with a family and a nice job in suburbia to scale a cliff? Why spend hundreds or even thousands of dollars to go to a place where you will get sick if you brush your teeth with the water?

When I first began to consider traveling to Thailand and Nepal on a pilgrimage, these are just a few of the questions that came to mind. Leaders Roy Oswald and Carol Rousch knew this would be the case, which is why they advised that prospective pilgrims begin a journal to record the process through which we would come to a decision. Our pilgrimage, they said, began with our clarifying why we wanted to go.

I should mention here that the world is divided into two types of people: those who write in journals and those who don't. I am in the group of those who don't, but I agreed to the process and began the journal in which I would record my impressions and experiences and dialogue with my "inner wisdom."

When I began to write in the journal, it was first to clarify whether or not I wanted to embark on this pilgrimage at all. It meant leaving home and being away from my husband, Chuck, for a few weeks. But more than that, it meant being in a place where we would be unable to communicate. Even when we are in the same town, Chuck has his cell phone with him, and there is hardly a minute of the day that we cannot pick up a telephone and check in with each other. And we do. Even after thirty-plus years of marriage, we rarely let a day go by without knowing what both of us are up to. So here I was, looking at one huge ten-day communication gap and a whole bunch of shorter ones and wondering, What if Chuck gets sick while I am up there in those mountains and I

don't even know about it and there he is alone, perhaps dying, and I am not with him? Or more likely, what if I get sick and die up there and all he gets is a body shipped back to him C.O.D.? Will it be worth it?

I found myself using the journal to catalogue these and other fears. In addition to my concerns about leaving home, I noticed that my travel trepidations fell into five different categories, with several focused on the various orifices of the body.

The first category was little invisible creatures in the food and water. I wrote, "I guess when you are a control freak, diarrhea is a basic symbol of being out of control. Needless to say, there is a lot in life that is not in control—everything, in fact, but I do persist in keeping up the illusion of some control."

Category two had to do with fears about how I would handle the discomforts and inconveniences of foreign travel. "Will I get cranky and become the Ugly American?" I wrote. "Chuck says I am a wuss. How much of a wuss am I really?" I feared meeting up with my not-so-wonderful self.

Category three I called "potty paranoia." How would I maintain any semblance of modesty on the ten-day trek in Nepal? There was no question that I would feel the urge on many occasions when there were no facilities available. I had it all figured out, though. I would wear my poncho and squat demurely in even the most uncivilized terrain.

My deepest fears were in category four. Our leaders told us there had been only two occasions when trekkers had to be lifted out in helicopters. One of them was a very stable man who had such a case of culture shock that it made him physically sick. He very literally found himself on the brink of death. I wondered if the smells and sites of poverty would overload the circuits of my psyche and convert my capacity for compassion into depression. When my husband went to India, he was incapacitated by a severe depression unlike anything he had experienced before or since. I once witnessed the near drowning of a man who had a sudden panic attack in a few feet of water, in spite of the fact that he was a very good swimmer. I was aware of how unpredictably the human emotional system can respond in situations both familiar and unfamiliar.

The fifth category was the question of physical endurance. Would my body handle this? I have arthritis in my neck, back, hips, and knees and a spur on my right foot—a great candidate for walking ten miles a day. And I don't do well in cold weather—my toes go numb at about 40 degrees Fahrenheit. Was it absurd, I wondered, to ask my body to perform beyond its limits? But then again, what were the limits? Would I know if I did not at least attempt to ask more of it?

With so many fears, I asked myself in the journal, why was I going? Partly to meet them, I said. To get out of my comfort zone.

I wanted to encounter the monsters; I wanted to get to know myself—my limits and my potential—more intimately. Instinctively, perhaps, I knew that the conditions most conducive to spiritual growth are not in the comfort zone but on the "growing edges," where faith meets fear, and the trust that emerges from that test of faith is grounded in what is true and good.

As it turned out, landing in Bangkok after twenty-some hours of travel and sleep deprivation gave me the opportunity early on to meet the fear of being the Ugly American, especially when it took an hour after getting to the hotel room to get my luggage. I did, in fact, get to see how cranky I could be, and I am sure that my demeanor toward the attendant in the luggage room transcended all language barriers. As Jon Kabat-Zinn writes, "Wherever you go, there you are."[2] Before I could fall asleep that evening, I had to return to the luggage room to offer an apology.

With so many fears, why was I going? Partly to meet them. To get out of my comfort zone. I wanted to encounter the monsters.

I was one of very few who didn't get sick on the trip—at least not until the flight home, when I discovered that some uninvited guests had stowed away in my body. Others in our group, however, were less fortunate.

At one point, I genuinely feared that one of our group would die before we could get medical assistance. It was our third night, and we camped at Ghorepani after hiking from an elevation of 5,000 feet to 9,100 feet. The climb was difficult enough for those of us who were healthy and in good shape, but there was one man who was quite ill. With help from the Sherpas and fellow pilgrims, he made the ascent; but that evening he passed out. The group formed a circle of support and healing for him and for ourselves. He made it through the night and finished the trek. For this we were all grateful. His grave illness, however, reminded us that you do not have to climb Mount Everest to endanger your life and health. Even on a tamer trek such as ours, you are a very long way from the nearest medical clinic, which is probably less than adequate by our first-world standards anyway. How spoiled we are, we who complain incessantly about our systems of health care! At least we have systems to complain about.

Living on the edge as we did, however, reminded us to attend to our spiritual needs and to come together as a community. We took time each morning after meditation and yoga and chanting to form a healing circle. Anyone who was feeling a need for support for any reason was invited to take his or her place in the middle, and we did a laying on of hands. That is, we touched the person and offered our prayers or hopes or blessings for his or her health and well-being. We were all walking pharmacies but ended up using very little of our prescription drugs. Most people recovered from their bouts of vomiting or diarrhea within a day. I

believe the healing circle made a difference. We live in a culture that is far too dependent on drugs. It is yet another symptom of our tendency to look for instant gratification, the quick fix; it is also an indication of our need to become more at home in our bodies. (In Chapter Four, I will have more to say about how we have become alienated from our bodies.)

As for my concerns for modesty, I dealt with those early on. In preparation for the rigors of hiking in the Himalayas, we went on a short trek to a primitive village in the hill tribe country of Thailand to help get into shape. All thirteen of us—six women and seven men—stayed overnight in a one-room bamboo hut and shared an outhouse that had a shred of blanket pretending to be a door. So much for modesty there.

In Nepal, where we women in particular wanted to show respect for a culture of modesty, it was sometimes a challenge. For example, when we were above the snow line in barren mountains, there was not so much as a bush for cover. I tried my poncho trick in thirty-mile-an-hour winds, and the Sherpas are still laughing about it. Sometimes the best antidote to fear is a sense of humor.

I was amazed at how much energy I had wasted on fear. Time after time, I found myself fearing I would not be able to do something. Then I would do it. I would just do it, and the grip of fear was released. There was more fear in the anticipation than in the reality of living, step by step.

I also encountered a fear in a category I had not anticipated. This was the fear of being robbed—particularly, of losing my passport. I did not like being distrustful; I did not like regarding the people of another culture as potential intruders. By the third week of the trip, I was much more relaxed and trusting, but it was a struggle, and I had some help from others in the group, who gently challenged me to get past this wall of distrust I had erected between myself and the people of Kathmandu.

I had confessed to my journal that I anticipated great difficulty handling the emotional shock of witnessing the suffering and impoverishment in Nepal. Though once again anticipation proved worse than the actual experience, I definitely felt out of my comfort zone, not just in Nepal but in Thailand as well. The Thai economy was quite depressed. Even in relatively cosmopolitan Bangkok, we flew over large partly constructed buildings that had been abandoned before completion—derelict denizens of a landscape scarred by economic collapse. Our flight took us north to Chiang Mai. During our stay in the north, we went for a short trek into the hill-tribe area. On the way, we stopped at a village for a snack. Women selling hand-woven hats and belts hounded us to purchase their wares, and if I bought something from one of them, several others pounced on me, desperately insistent that I needed theirs as well.

In several places along our trekking path, we breathed the smoke from fires that consumed the drought-scorched forest. We

were told that these were deliberately set by hunters to flush out the animals. After about three hours, we arrived in the primitive Karin village where we spent the night. There people lived at subsistence level but seemed less desperate. Some, however, had resorted to selling drugs to tourists, as we discovered when the military police raided the village at dawn to make an arrest. We were treated to an elephant ride and rafted down the river on bamboo floats, but we did not enjoy these pursuits of privilege without an awareness that our hosts were struggling each day to feed themselves and their families.

I was overwhelmed by the signs of poverty in Nepal, one of the world's poorest and least developed nations. Particularly in Kathmandu, the filth and pollution were heartbreaking. This description written by Lu Anne Patrick, a fellow pilgrim, offers a few images from an evening in the city:

> Walking in Kathmandu by myself at twilight, it is so overstimulating to me. I can barely function. The streets are alive with so much color, waving prayer flags, flapping material from store fronts and strange architecture; the sounds of car horns blaring and foreign tongues yelling, then the smells of dirt and exhaust and garbage and animals. I try to stay focused but keep getting lost in first one thing, then another. A man steps out his door with a goat

behind him, turns, takes a large knife out of his back pocket, and slits the goat's throat and disembowels it right in front of me. An old woman bends over, blows her nose out one side, and flings a four-foot line of snot into the air. I just cannot seem to gather all this in. Each sense and its messages overwhelm me, and receiving these sensory messages all together, I am lost. I walk on, and suddenly I am within an inch of stepping on this live "thing" in the gutter. I freeze, and all time stops. All sounds fade, and like a frozen frame in a movie, nothing exists but this human creature lying in the gutter. He is twisted, pretzel-like, in the garbage on the road. His limbs are grotesquely wound together like two bike frames that have been flung off the back of a car going seventy-five miles an hour on the freeway. From one very thin and crippled hand he rings a little bell. Ting, ting, ting. He wears a filthy diaper and nothing else. I stand frozen, and his eyes meet mine in this frozen picture frame. We stand for an eternity in this silent space of eyes and humanity. My God, who is this man? Suddenly the sounds, smells, sights come rushing back, and I move on into the gathering darkness. Long after I turn the corner, I hear the ting, ting of his little bell.

It would have been easy to shield ourselves from the pain of

witnessing these things. But we were not there to run away from pain; we were there to cultivate our compassion. *Namaste* was the common greeting among people in Nepal. It was said with a gentleness that communicated "the Divine/Spirit within me greets the Divine/Spirit within you." Repeating this beautiful phrase dozens of time a day, we were invited to recognize the divine in each person rather than turn away from what is painful or repugnant.

I was also impressed with the genuine hospitality of the people. On one occasion, while I was in the large square where hundreds of vendors market their crafts (and many blocks away from our hotel), I asked one of the merchants where I might find a toilet, and he led me into a building and down some stairs to a typical toilet facility. He took a key from his pocket and opened the door. When I came out, I found him there guarding my privacy and waiting to relock the door; I realized then that he had taken me to his home. It would have been out of the question back in the United States to ask to use a stranger's private facilities, let alone to be accommodated with such a natural and unconsciously genuine charity.

Our primary interaction with Nepali people was with our band of Sherpa guides and porters. Besides appreciating their attentive service and delicious meals, my chief recollection is of their ready laughter, their multiverse folksongs, and their exuberant dancing. Their camaraderie and hospitality graciously blessed our entire trip. One evening, they baked a cake for a member of our group who was having a birthday, decorated it, and presented it with pride, insisting that we also sample a special apple brandy from the region where we were camped. Since they had no oven facilities on the trail, they had gone to considerable effort to make the cake over an open fire.

On our last evening in Kathmandu, after we returned from the trek, our Sherpa guides hosted a dinner for us in the home of our head Sherpa, Lakpa. He and his wife and four children lived there in two rooms, another family of three lived in a third room, and they all shared a bathroom, which consisted of a hole in the floor with a small porcelain slab, a bucket of water, and (in deference to their Western visitors) a roll of toilet paper. On another floor of their building was a small and primitive kitchen out of which they prepared wonderful and amazing food. The daughters washed dishes from a faucet on the rooftop deck outside the kitchen. About twenty of us gathered in the two small but attractive rooms, where cots lined the walls and doubled as both chairs and beds. Seated on the cots, we could easily reach the table in the center, which was heaped with generous portions of popcorn and fried vegetable appetizers before we were served a four-course meal. An entire wall of one room of this precious space was dedicated to a Buddhist shrine featuring butter lamps, images of the Buddha, and a photograph of the Dalai Lama. Although these people were

poor by our standards, they were much better off than most of the city dwellers, and they obviously enjoyed hosting us, exhibiting a gracious spirit of generosity. Once again I was struck by the notion that those who have little share much and, in contrast, those who have much share little.

❧

I was not the only pilgrim in our group who was out of her comfort zone. Each of us was assigned a buddy to keep up with, and mine was Jane Ellen, a lovely southern woman—bright, pleasant, and pretty. She dressed immaculately, her makeup was perfect, and every hair was in place.

Everyone in our group had trained for the physical rigors of our journey, and our initial short trek in Thailand was the test of our training. Our guides equipped us with the packs and sleeping bags we would need for our overnight stay in the hills. For many in our group who were not accustomed to backpacking, even this light pack was a burden. The day turned out incredibly hot and humid, and the terrain was steep and slippery.

For Jane Ellen, this half-day hike pushed the limits of her endurance. After we returned to our comfortable hotel in Chiang Mai, she told me she did not think she would be able to do the Nepal trek. She had had a very hard time, not only with the physical challenges of the hike, but also with the effects of weather, dirt, and the lack of privacy for personal care. She was meeting up with some of her own monsters, particularly her need to feel in control, and it was a painful encounter. I told her about Parker Palmer's experience with Outward Bound. "If you can't get out of it, get into it," I said, encouraging her to allow her soul its inner tussle with the spirit, to "ride the monsters all the way down," as Palmer had put it. I also told her that if it did not feel safe to get into it at that particular time and she chose not to go on the Nepal trek, it would be all right. Others in the group also held her in their care as she struggled with her fear.

So Jane Ellen rode with her monsters. She named the fear, got into the fear, and came through it. She wrote later of this experience:

> I went on the 1998 spiritual pilgrimage to Thailand and Nepal, in part, to wrench myself from my comfortable middle-class existence and face life on more fundamental terms. In other words, I purposely stepped outside my comfort zone, believing that I would learn things about myself—and perhaps call on things within myself—that I would not have the opportunity to do in my day-to-day life.
>
> I got what I wanted in spades. Our first trek began in the hill country of Thailand near Chiang Mai. We strapped on our packs and started out in the heat of the day. It

didn't take me long to realize that those two elements—carrying a pack and weathering the heat—were going to be enormous challenges for me. I quickly asked for help with the pack and somehow trudged on, lightheaded and nauseous.

I reached the Karin village still standing but very fearful of the larger trek that lay ahead in Nepal. The day after we returned from the village, I was seized with severe anxiety. The trek in Nepal required hiking eight to ten miles a day for ten days. I was not at all sure that I could do it. I was also not sure how well I would do in primitive conditions. I had never slept in a tent. I had never bathed with a bowl of water. I feared sickness from unfamiliar food. It was a difficult time.

I voiced my fears to Sarah, who told me about the Outward Bound motto: "If you can't get out of it, get into it." This echoed a message I had received from a woman whom I greatly admire. Now the chancellor of a major university, she spoke of an intern experience with the U.S. Forest Service in which she was taught one of the basics when battling forest fires: When the fire threatens to overtake you, don't run from it. Instead, rush through the fire line to the side that has already been burned. The same message: the only way out is through.

Another message surfaced as I wrestled with my anxiety: I read once that fear is the opposite of love. This trek proved that to me. I honestly believe that it was the goodwill of the group—their prayers, their kind comments, their advice and support—that gave me the courage to go on the trek in spite of my fears.

It is difficult for me to let go of control and trust myself to the universe. But that's exactly what I had to do in Nepal. I found myself at one point saying, "I hope this doesn't kill me." Then I realized that that really was the whole point, at least metaphorically. As a Christian, I believe that you have to go through Good Friday if you want to get to Easter.

My fear had to give way to trust. Something in me had to die for new life to emerge.

As I entered the final hours of the trek, I was conscious of the sun on my face and the wind at my back. I remembered the Irish blessing and felt blessed indeed. I also consciously realized that I was following Kandu (yes, pronounced "can do"), our head Sherpa's wife, who had walked by my side for nearly the entire trek. She was an uncommonly strong woman with a can-do spirit who could sense the needs of others. I will be forever thankful for her presence.

The other thought that coursed through my brain as I neared Jomsom and the end of the trek was a line from William Faulkner's speech when he accepted the Nobel Prize. He said that humankind will not only endure; we will prevail. I felt that somehow I had more than endured the trek. I had prevailed.

But I clearly had not done it alone. I was surrounded by love—by the many kindnesses of the group and the care of Kandu and the Sherpas. Their support helped me work through my fears and learn firsthand that the only way out is through.

Jane Ellen made the trek with courage and grace, exhibiting a strength that was an inspiration to others. And she realized what the rest of us knew—that she was quite beautiful even without makeup.

Although Jane Ellen's fears were different from mine and from those of others who traveled in our group, the context of the pilgrimage, with its intentional commitment to both spiritual growth and a deepening of community, created a safe environment for her to explore her growing edges. This was an aspect of pilgrimage that allowed fears to surface and be engaged. When we leave the comfort zone, we should not be abandoned to struggle with the monsters alone. Pilgrimage, with its invitation to a time that is "betwixt and between" the events of our structured and time-driven lives, is by nature a time of vulnerability. Thus we must create a holding environment that is caring, compassionate, and open to the urgings of the spirit toward freedom, truth, and hope. In that safe but vulnerable space, the pilgrim is free to explore the shadow places in the landscape of the solitary soul.

The pilgrimage to Thailand and Nepal was the highlight of my six-month sabbatical. During that time, I also traveled to Scotland in late spring, to the beautiful and sacred island of Celtic tradition, Iona. I encountered some fears there, too, although I did not anticipate them. I knew that Scotland was not going to give me culture shock and that the water was safe. And there was no question of distrust: Iona was a place without locks. We were told that we wouldn't need keys to our rooms; no one ever locked doors on Iona. I felt a sense of safety there like I have never experienced anywhere, and it stirred me with a longing for the kind of human community where there is no need for locks. A woman in our group had once been the victim of a violent attack, and she spoke tearfully and gratefully of being able to go outside at night for the first time in two years. She knew that the feeling of safety was as much inside herself as it was in her environment, but being in a safe place helped her get past the fear that had deprived her of her nighttime freedom.

On most days, we attended a seminar in the morning and then explored the island in the afternoon. One day was set aside for silence and solitude. We were not to talk with one another until we met in the evening in a small chapel for singing. I knew what I wanted to do with my day: I wanted to explore the south end of Iona, the wildest part of the island. Vivienne Hull, one of our leaders, advised me not to go there alone because I could get there only by passing through a narrow passageway at low tide and could get out only by climbing the cliff in a particular spot. I would need a guide. But I went anyway.

It was exhilarating to be out there alone. I knew this was a safe island, but I was also aware that it was out of my comfort zone. My discomfort rose dramatically when I could not find the place in the cliff where I could get out. It was raining, and the ground was slippery. I began to feel a little panic and wonder if the tide had closed off the gap yet. I felt stupid. I could slip and get hurt and no one was near. It was then that I knew why Vivienne had said that I would need a guide. From these humbling moments, I learned why a guide is always an essential element of a pilgrimage adventure. When you enter a wilderness space—when you cross the threshold into liminal space—someone has to provide the anchor in real time while you exercise your freedom to be in another dimension of time and space. Also, in the practical sense, it helps to have someone who knows the territory.

As I sought to address my mounting anxiety, I told myself, "It's raining. You're getting wet. Just be wet, Sarah. The way out is here. You will find it. 'If you can't get out of it, get into it.'" I also assured myself that Vivienne would figure out that I had ventured where she had advised me not to go and would initiate a search for the prodigal pilgrim if I did not get back by the dinner hour.

I did find my way out. I hiked over to a beach and found a rock overhang for shelter and ate my lunch, then headed toward another part of the south end of the island that I had not yet explored. Just then, another woman in our group approached me. I was annoyed at first that she was going to break the covenantal silence. Then I realized that she was in tears, very upset. She was lost and was terrified. There were no clear paths on the island. She needed help. So I helped her find her way back and resumed my wandering, feeling pretty good that I had been able to find my own way and guide her.

From these humbling moments, I learned why a guide is always an essential element of a pilgrimage adventure. . . . Someone has to provide the anchor in real time while you exercise your freedom to be in another dimension of time and space.

"Pride goeth before a fall," they say, and it wasn't long before I took my tumble.

I had no compass. You don't need a compass on a little island where you can see the coast. But the rain and fog had gotten

heavier—what coast? It was just heather and bogs—lots of bogs, where one step in the deceptive terrain took me knee deep into the muck. I thought of *Pilgrim's Progress* and the Slough of Despond. I was lost—really lost. All I could do was walk in one direction or another until I hit the coast. As panic began erupting again in my soggy spirit, I kept repeating that mantra: "If you can't get out of it, get into it." I told myself, "You're lost, Sarah. Just be lost." "Getting into it" meant allowing myself to wander in the bogs without knowing whether I was going in the right direction. It meant realizing I was, in fact, going in the wrong direction and had to go back and start off in another direction, not once but twice. It meant feeling fear in the chill that seeped through my clothing to my skin and to my bones. Most of all, it meant moving, even when I did not know where I was going, and trusting that yes, I would find my way "home."

Eventually, I found my way back, wet and cold. Vivienne and Sharon Daloz Parks (the other leader) had given us all a booklet of readings for the week, and I came across a poem by David Wagoner. The title caught my eye. It's called "Lost." I ended up putting it on a postcard of an aerial view of the island. Where he used the words *forest* and *trees,* I substituted *bogs* and *heather.*

Stand still. The trees ahead and the bushes beside you
Are not lost. Wherever you are is called Here,
And you must treat it as a powerful stranger,
Must ask permission to know it and be known.
The forest breathes. Listen. It answers,
I have made this place around you.
If you leave it, you may come back again, saying Here.
No two trees are the same to Raven.
No two branches are the same to Wren.
If what a tree or a bush does is lost on you,
You are surely lost. Stand still. The forest knows
Where you are. You must let it find you.[3]

The poem gave deeper meaning to my experience and gave me permission to be lost—to feel at home in the strangeness, to feel safe in the wildness. It gave me permission to have no particular direction, to be wet, to be lost, to be afraid. More than that, it reminded me why I was there. The poem spoke directly to me: If what a tree or bush—or heather or bog—does is lost on you, you are surely lost. I had not just deepened my respect for an alien landscape; I had befriended the bog as "a powerful stranger."

In one of our seminars, Sharon asked, "How do we know that God is with us?" And she answered, "We know because we will be led to places we did not plan to go."[4]

We know because we will be led to places we did not plan to go. Yes—

- Places inside ourselves, where we meet our fears and ride the monsters down
- Places that warn us against adapting too much to our surroundings, that warn against adapting to a world where we numb our own pain and shield ourselves from the pain of others
- Places where we might get lost, where we do not have control
- Places where we take risks and find out we can do things we didn't know we could do
- Places where we discover a deeper self, a higher self, a *better* self
- Places where we meet each other and touch because we are companions on this journey—each of us lost

Our fears take us to the edge of our being, to a place where we are fully alive. Whatever the fear—whether you are an arthritic climbing a mountain, a hiker lost on an island, a traveler in a strange city, or a shy person facing lunch hour in a new job—it takes you to the edge. This is the point of every self-help book you will ever read.

But the edge is a scary place—risky and dangerous. You can lose yourself there.

The edge is also where creativity is generated. We think of insanity as being out of touch with reality, when in fact it is sometimes really a matter of being too much in touch with reality. Henry Miller wrote, "A good artist must have a streak of insanity . . . if by insanity is meant an exaggerated inability to adapt."[5]

If you are fully alive, you wrestle with the monsters of your own fear, you are willing to venture to the edge, and you may have something of an inability to adapt.

> *"Our doubts are traitors*
> *And make us lose the good we oft might win*
> *By fearing to attempt."*
>
> —Spoken by Lucio the Clown in *Measure for Measure*, William Shakespeare

In her novel *The Stone Diaries,* Carol Shields identified what happens when we adapt too well—when we allow ourselves to become too comfortable. "The larger loneliness of our lives," she wrote, "evolves from our unwillingness to spend ourselves, stir ourselves. We are always damping down our inner weather, permitting ourselves the comforts of postponement, or rehearsals."[6]

Shields's image of "damping down our inner weather" is one of allowing our lives to live us instead of living our lives. Too much of life is spent avoiding ourselves—avoiding our feelings, avoiding

intimate relationships, and avoiding the deep and meaningful connections that the spirit longs for. The larger loneliness of our lives is our avoidance of life.

I am reminded of the illustration of the frog in the pot of boiling water. I've never tried this to see if it is true, but I hear that if you put a frog in a pot of boiling water, it will jump out before it cooks. But if you put the frog in a pot of cold water and gradually raise the temperature, it will adapt to the heat. Before it realizes what has happened, it has been dressed with garlic butter and is entertaining someone's gourmet palate.

The ability to adapt, then, can numb you to life—to what is real and true. As the frog's fate illustrates, it can also have deadly consequences.

I recall speaking with Suzanne, a woman who was unhappy with her marriage. She loved her husband, and they got along well. They had two children still in school. His decision to embark on a career creating computer software had coincided with the phenomenal growth in the industry, and his earnings provided for a lifestyle that included exotic travel, fine dining, and evenings at the theater or opera. A small-town girl from Colorado, Suzanne enjoyed decorating her spacious suburban home, playing tennis at the country club, and volunteering for the Hospice Auxiliary. She was often depressed, however, and felt that her own creative energy was stifled. Although she and her husband seemed to have little in common besides the children, he was a decent person, and she had decided to accept a relationship of convenience that was affectionate but not sexual. She confessed that she was not willing to give up financial security and a very comfortable lifestyle in order to respond to her inner tug for more meaningful self-expression.

While her children were still in high school, Suzanne developed a serious drinking problem. After her family intervened, she sought treatment and joined Alcoholics Anonymous. Once sober, she realized how she had gradually allowed herself to adapt to a way of being that was very literally killing her. She had damped down her inner weather and permitted herself the comfort of postponement for too long. She summoned the courage to "get out of the pot" before it was too late and addressed her fears of financial insecurity. Training for a career in health care, she found satisfying employment. After a brief period of separation from her husband, she recognized that her dissatisfaction with her marriage was rooted more in her fears than in the relationship. Freed from the fears, she reentered the marriage, where she and her husband grew in a mutual love and respect they had never previously experienced.

Jumping out of the pot when it is comfortable takes a little extra courage, but we do not grow personally or spiritually if we stay in our comfort zone. Neither do we grow when the fear of change silences our inner cry for freedom or deadens our capacity to respond to an inner voice of wisdom and compassion.

We "lead lives of quiet desperation," wrote Thoreau, in his classic book chronicling his pilgrim-time at Walden Pond,[7] where he immersed himself in nature's classroom in an effort to live deliberately, to be fully awake. "Brain-rot" is what he called our human inclination toward petty distraction and our enmeshment in the world of material things.

Leaving the comfort zone is an invitation to become free of the fears that prevent us from exploring our own human depths. In the conclusion to *Walden,* Thoreau wrote, "If you would learn to speak all tongues and conform to the customs of all nations, if you would travel farther than all travelers, be naturalized in all climes, and cause the Sphinx to dash her head against a stone, even obey the precept of the old philosopher, and Explore thyself. Herein are demanded the eye and the nerve."[8]

Yes, leaving the comfort zone calls for a quickening of the eye and the nerve, and the journey inward ultimately opens you to a more comfortable relationship with the outer world in which you make your home. Thoreau gives us this rhyme for our pilgrim travels at home and abroad:

> Direct your eye right inward, and you'll find
> A thousand regions in your mind
> Yet undiscovered. Travel them, and be
> Expert in home-cosmography.[9]

chapter three

At Home in the Wilderness Within

It is easier to sail many thousands of miles through cold and storm and cannibals, in a government ship, with five hundred men and boys to assist one, than it is to explore the private sea, the Atlantic and Pacific of one's being alone.

—Henry David Thoreau

In the charming and fanciful Maurice Sendak story *Where the Wild Things Are,* young Max wore his wolf suit and got into various kinds of mischief until his mother called him "WILD THING!" Max threatened to eat her up and was sent off to bed without his supper. That night, a forest grew in his room, then an ocean tumbled by, and Max boarded a boat and "sailed off through night and day and in and out of weeks . . . to where the wild things are." The wild things "gnashed their terrible teeth and rolled their terrible eyes and showed their terrible claws," but Max tamed them, and they made him king of the wild things. Even though they gave him the power to rule them and to send them off to bed without their supper, Max was lonely and wanted to go home. The wild things tried to scare him into staying, but he "sailed back over a year and in and out of weeks and through a day and into the night of his very own room where he found his supper waiting for him . . . and it was still hot."[1]

From the time we are children, we go on journeys real and imaginary into the places of our dreams, our lives, and our world where the wild things are—where we face our fears or struggle to understand who we are in relationship to others who inhabit our world, where we do battle more with the monsters within us than with those around us. Max's journey follows the pilgrim theme, which takes one across the threshold that divides yesterday from today and today from tomorrow and turns the hierarchy of power in relationships upside down. In the land of the wild things, Max not only tames the terrible beasts, but he enters the place in his own lonely heart that wants to return home. So he sails back across time into his own room, where nothing has changed except him.

Wilderness is part of every personal journey and part of our journey together as human beings who seek to live in relationship with one another and with the wildness of our vast and awesome universe. To enter the wilderness is to sail across oceans of time and space and make friends with the wild things that haunt our dreams or inhabit our physical environment. There we tame our fears and are tamed by them.

The pilgrim journey into wilderness reminds us that we are alone and not alone. We are neither where we have been nor where we are going. There is danger and possibility, risk and promise. We leave seeking spiritual peace but are confronted by discoveries that we did not pursue, that may disturb or baffle us. We may choose to enter wilderness like the Hebrew slaves who followed Moses out of Egypt, to escape bondage, or like Henry David Thoreau, to "live deliberately." Or we may, like Jesus and his forty days of encountering Satan, be driven there seemingly without choice. Once on our journey, our markers of time and space collapse, for this wilderness is not in space or time but is the boundless territory of the soul.

To enter the wilderness is to sail across oceans of time and space and make friends with the wild things that haunt our dreams or inhabit our physical environment.

Time in wilderness, however, is not some romantic pleasure trip. It is the heart of pilgrimage and is always a time of struggle. I knew this when I embarked on my pilgrim adventures to foreign lands, but knowing that you can expect to struggle is not the same as being in the midst of it. It is all very well to say you are open to pain as well as joy, but you may change your mind when you are living with the pain.

Wilderness is where you expect the unexpected, even if you set out with your map and compass and a clear statement of intention—even if you have searched your soul, researched your goal, and employed a guide. In fact, every bit of preparation you have made enhances your chances of meeting up with mystery, flirting with the accidental, and inviting serendipity—ever aware of the possibility of misfortune.

One of the hardest journeys I took was not to an exotic foreign land but to a place that I had thought of as a sort of home. In 1998, I spent a month in the mountains of North Carolina, where my brother and I still owned a parcel of pastured and wooded land on which our parents and our younger brother had lived and died in the 1980s. In the house on the property, we had left the furnishings and much of the decorating so that we had the option of visiting or hosting friends there in addition to renting.

Wilderness is where you expect the unexpected, even if you set out with your map and compass and a clear statement of intention.

It was in that house that my husband's son Tom, who was staying there for a few months, decided to end his life in January 1998. He was twenty-eight and had been troubled for many years with depression. The mission for my journey home, a little over two months after Tom's death, was to clean out the house and prepare it to be leased unfurnished.

Included in the emotional knapsack that I carried into the house with me was anger at Tom, whose suicide defiled a home that held so many warm memories. I was surprised, however, at how quickly my anger dissipated. The house was haunted, yes, and some of its haunting was his pain and despair, but it was also haunted with his loving attention to the grounds, his duct-tape repairs, and his dogged plugging of potholes in the road. If he spoke to me there, it was to say, "Thank you for giving me a safe place to be with my pain." I wept for him and found my anger replaced with an invitation to him to linger awhile longer if he wished.

Next I purchased a bundle of white sage and performed a ritual of purification and blessing. In each room of the house, using a hawk's feather to fan the smoking embers of the sage into the space, I breathed in the aroma of its cleansing and spoke of the memories, real and imagined, held by the space. A previous renter had abused the house, so I purged it of whatever power the abuser may have claimed in my own psyche. In the room where Tom had chosen his death, I offered a prayer of blessing for his tortured spirit and a benediction of peace upon the place where he had found peace on his own terms.

I then dismantled the house and prepared for the yard sale of the century. Everything that had gone up into the attic years before now came down for the process of deciding what to keep, what to sell, what to give away, and what to toss. As anyone knows who has ever sorted through the belongings of someone after a death (in this case, a series of deaths), the process of dismantling a house is a pilgrimage in itself. In this case, it was layered with fifteen years of memory.

"Home is where the grief is," I wrote in my journal after unearthing old family photographs that had remained in the piano bench and discovering a box of precious items that had mistakenly been stored away in the attic all these years. Among the buried treasures was a carved wooden figure sculpted by my mother. Standing about a foot high, it was of a woman whose head was bowed but whose arms stretched upward and outward, with hands—wonderful hands—open. It was a curious gift, this figure whose pain-etched face looked down while her arms opened skyward.

Reluctantly, I packed my old vinyl LPs to take to a local record dealer, but not before playing the Doors' version of "Light My Fire" on the old console phonograph that not even the Salvation

Army wanted. I kept *The Circle Game* by Tom Rush and my recording of Dylan Thomas reading his poetry, even though we no longer had any equipment for playing records. Going through books on the shelves, I found marginal notes and news clippings, ghostly whisperings from brittle yellowed pages.

A friend observed that I seemed to enjoy playing store as I arranged items for sale on shelves in the pantry and invited everyone I knew to come shopping. Every time friends or neighbors left the house with their bargain booty, I felt a burden lifted. The Quakers call it "cumber," all this stuff that we accumulate. How freeing it was to let it all go. Even when strangers purchased my mother's crewel-embroidered pillow covers at the giant yard sale in which the great purge of possessions culminated, it felt like a gift to know that these items that had been gathering dust in the attic would be enjoyed.

Piece by piece, many of the house's furnishings and appliances were carried out during the last week of my sojourn. A moving company then cleared the house of the items my brother and I wanted to take back to California.

Before leaving the house, I relighted the bundle of white sage and walked through the empty rooms. I did not know when—or if—I would return. The house was leased, so I had given up the option of visiting. This time, my prayers and blessings were of gratitude for the past and good wishes for those who would occupy these rooms in the future. I left the bundle in the fireplace, still smoldering, and walked out the door.

Curiously, it was in the process of letting go of the house, its hauntings, and its contents that I had reclaimed it. In leaving this home, I had made it more homelike. In entering the wilderness of feelings that I brought with me when I arrived, I moved through anger to forgiveness and love. Although I did not know it at the time, events in my life would change dramatically, and I would return a year later to take up residence myself.

I was also unaware of how this process of dismantling a house and making peace with my stepson was preparation for the Iona pilgrimage that followed directly after that time.

You will recall from Chapter Two that people go to the Scottish island of Iona because of its special qualities as a wild, dark, natural place, a place of contemplation, a place where one feels "at home" as part of nature's larger scheme. It has been called "a wild place on the edge of time." It is a place where the veil between the seen and the unseen worlds is thinner, where the kind of mystical connection we often associate with spirituality in all traditions is commonplace and faeries are said to transport people from the world

> *"All wilderness seems to be full of tricks and plans to drive and draw us up into God's light."*
>
> —John Muir, *My First Summer in the Sierra*

of the seen to the world of the unseen. I like the story of an old Irish countrywoman who was confronted by a Roman priest. "Do you believe in faeries?" he asked. "I do not," she answered, "but they're there."[2]

The mystical is part of everyday life there. Every family has someone with second sight. They can move into the unseen world and back again. They might say, "Aunt Vi is having a wee spell," or "She's gone over the hedge again."

Even though I don't believe in faeries either, I experienced something extraordinary while sojourning on Iona. I went there, as you may recall, for a women's spirituality retreat. My husband, Chuck, was working in England at the time, so he met up with me in Scotland and went with me to Iona. Since my hotel was reserved for women only, he checked into lodgings nearby and planned to leave early the next morning. The retreat did not begin until evening, so we had about two hours to take a walk shortly after we arrived. We went first to the abbey, where Chuck lit a candle for Tom before we walked toward the north end of the island. Menacing black thunderheads billowed above and sputtered the first harbingers of a serious storm. I suggested that we needed to turn back, but Chuck kept going, a man on a mission. In retrospect, I think he was having a wee spell. He did not know why, but he was drawn out to a rocky point at the north beach. When he got as far as he could go, he took a stone he had picked up earlier and tossed it out into the sea. He told me he felt a mysterious urge to leave a symbol of Tom there with his Scottish ancestors (his Campbell clan had come from the Argyll region). The clouds exploded as we started back, and we both ended up drenched.

I didn't tell any of the women in our group about this incident until I heard about something that happened to one of them. Elsa was the mother of a young man in his twenties who had made several suicide attempts. On the day that we all spent in solitude and silence, Elsa chose to go to the north beach, where, for reasons she could not explain, she picked up a rock, went out to the farthest point, and threw it into the sea. She said it was a symbol of letting go of being able to control what her son chose to do with his life. It was a gesture of freedom for her.

Before I went to Iona, I read a book about a woman's pilgrimage to Celtic sacred sites called *Crossing to Avalon,* given to me by my friend Amelia, who had died the same day as my stepson Tom. In the book, Jean Bolen writes: "In fairy tales, legends, and science fiction, the main character often arrives at a 'gateway' that is [special]. Here and now, she or he must choose whether to step through and go beyond the known world. . . . The idea of passing through a gateway . . . is reflected in the . . . word *liminality,* . . . meaning 'threshold.'" The author goes on to say that in liminal times such as transitions, we are thin-skinned and vulnerable, like

a snake when it molts its skin and is temporarily blind. In this state, the invisible spiritual world and visible reality come together.[3] We are open to synchronicity, a word Carl Jung used to name coincidences between our inner subjective world and outer events. Synchronicity is what happened on Iona: the invisible spiritual world and visible reality met. Liminal space invited these parents to give their pain to the rock and give the rock to the sea. And the sea and the rock and the divine and human spirits of the island offered healing for their aching hearts. Perhaps the landscape of the island became the landscape of the soul, rooted in a spirit-filled world that is blessed and timeless.

For me, this extraordinary event, coupled with the rituals of dismantling my haunted family home, opened my heart to an unanticipated wilderness struggle. For during the days that followed Chuck's gesture of symbolically bringing Tom's spirit to his ancestral home, I encountered a loss I had not named among those I had already grieved. Once I had removed the insulating armor of my anger and genuinely blessed Tom's dear spirit, a deeper loss came crashing in. As a stepmother, I had loved Tom and his older brother unconditionally. They had both come to live

In liminal times such as transitions, we are thin-skinned and vulnerable, like a snake when it molts its skin and is temporarily blind. In this state, the invisible spiritual world and visible reality come together.

with us as teenagers, which is when the unconditional nature of my love was put to a rigorous test. In the wilderness that day, I faced the raw reality of what it meant to love someone without the expectation that your love will be returned. Worse than that, however, was what it had done to me, this gift to them of unconditional love. I was so good at it that I did not need the love that I had so magnanimously excused them from giving. My love had become a protection against needing the love I so feared would not be offered. My strength, it seemed, was my chief obstacle to a loving relationship. What I had called unconditional love was not, after all, unconditional, for I had placed a significant condition on myself.

If anyone had told me that my pilgrimage to Iona would take me into the wilderness of my own inadequate loving, I would have scoffed. Getting lost on the island, facing my fears, experiencing physical discomfort—these were conceivable trials. But recognizing my complicity in my own grief—that was not on the pilgrim itinerary. The result of my struggle, however, was a startling freedom from the noble love in which I had been stuck and an open path to more honest ways of loving.

Other shadows chased me through my pilgrim adventures, but not without ample light from the surrounding landscape to open my heart to what they may have to teach. Each time I met them, however, their power diminished. Indeed, it was in the wilderness,

where I struggled with them, that they became my soul-teachers instead of my soul-stalkers.

My friend Carolyn once told me of a pilgrimage she took with a group from her church to the cathedral of Chartres in France. For several weeks before the trip, they met with their minister in preparation for the journey, which would culminate with their walking the labyrinth in the center of the nave of the cathedral. Weaving in a quartered spiral pattern, the path of the labyrinth has been worn for almost eight centuries by bare pilgrim knees or feet, a body prayer and a journey, a transforming walk into the still center of divine mystery. The coils of the labyrinth lead to the center, but one must journey in and out, in and out, nearing and within sight of the goal but not reaching it, trusting that the winding path moves through its twists and turns toward the center. Once there, the pilgrim's path returns, not directly out of the coiled circle but back through the same route. The circuitous nature of the labyrinth's path, like rituals of circumambulation that are part of other pilgrimage traditions, is a meditation of centering the self in the Divine Self, of entering an empty center in order to be Spirit-filled.

Carolyn had walked the canvas replica charted in purple paint at her church. She was acquainted with the three stages of the walk: releasing (letting go of the details of life to quiet the empty mind), illumination (receiving energy, new insight, or whatever is in the center for the individual pilgrim), and union (joining God by joining the inner and outer worlds).[4] Though she had always derived inspiration from the ritual, she was particularly excited about walking the labyrinth at Chartres.

Her pilgrim group arrived at the cathedral in the early morning before the doors opened. The first worshipers to enter, they walked silently to the labyrinth, removed their shoes, and took their places in a prayerful queue. It was not long, however, before tourists swarmed about, many of them strolling thoughtlessly into the labyrinth to get a full view of the stained glass windows in the nave. Walking the first stage and quieting the mind in that context felt, Carolyn thought, something like trying to meditate on the scrimmage line at a football game. Instead of moving into a meditative mode, she felt agitated. As she finally neared the center, she recognized how superior she felt, she who understood the meaning of the labyrinth while the insensitive tourists snapping photographs seemed out of touch with the significance of where they stood. Although she had followed the serpentine path into the center with her face down most of the way, she wound her way out from the center looking up into the faces of those intrusive tourists. In the center, Carolyn had received something that enabled her to leave her irritation and her pious suit of armor there, emerging into the crowd with a smile.

In her book *When Things Fall Apart,* Buddhist nun Pema Chödrön relates the story of the Buddha, who sat under a tree on

the night during which he was to attain enlightenment. While he sat there, the demon forces of Mara attacked him. "The story goes," she writes, "that they shot swords and arrows at him, and that their weapons turned into flowers."

Chödrön offers her explanation of the story. "What does this story mean? My understanding of it is that what we habitually regard as obstacles are not really our enemies, but rather our friends. What we call obstacles are really the way the world and our entire experience teach us where we're stuck."[5]

My friend Carolyn's disappointment in the experience of the labyrinth ended up being the epiphany of the wilderness, where her walk into the presence of God gave her the ability to turn arrows into flowers and then to turn back to the tourist-infested nave with flowers to give.

Expect the unexpected. The first definition of a pilgrim offered in the *Oxford English Dictionary* establishes that a pilgrim is a stranger encountering the strange. A pilgrim is "one not at home," "a stranger," "a wayfarer, traveler, wanderer." In the second definition, a pilgrim is "one who journeys, usually a long distance, to some sacred place as an act of religious devotion."[6]

The first of these definitions captures the essence of the pilgrim heart, even when the journey is taken according to the criteria of the second, more specific definition. A pilgrim is "one not at home," but I would contend that the pilgrim heart is where one becomes at home with being not at home; that is, the pilgrim heart is at home in the strangeness of the wilderness.

At the core of the struggles that we may encounter personally while sojourning in our own wildernesses is our longing to align ourselves with what is strange and other in such a way that we fully understand and feel ourselves existing in a relationship of harmony with it. In our solitary struggles, we deepen our sense of connection with others. In our encounters with strangeness, we befriend what is other. We are perhaps always at odds with both our instinctively devised shells of self-protection as well as our socially created separations, but in our pilgrim ventures we are most receptive to the Spirit's voice, reminding us that we do indeed have a place in it all. In it, mind you, not above it looking down or outside looking in, but inside, where there is no looking, only seeing.

A pilgrim is "one not at home," but I would contend that the pilgrim heart is where one becomes at home with being not at home; that is, the pilgrim heart is at home in the strangeness of the wilderness.

My next-door neighbor is an artist; she paints from nature on very large canvases. Her paintings, however, are not landscapes. You do not view them; you are in them, intimately experiencing the subtle shades of an autumn leaf, the misty spray of a waterfall, the icy edge of a snow-rimmed creek, or the simple

statement of a bare birch twig against the December sky. As large as she works, she does not give you the big picture. Or does she? Perhaps what she does not give you is distance. The big picture, it turns out, is in the center.

Placing herself in the center of a desert landscape was a literal pilgrimage for Maureen Killoran, a Unitarian Universalist minister. As part of a Wisdom Quest in Utah, she was sent out into the wilderness of the desert to spend more than three days in a "solo site" of her own selection. Later she recalled, "I hung off the edge of a rubbly ledge to secure my tarpaulin against the canyon winds. Never having mastered the 'slip knot' that makes things infinitely adjustable, I tied and tied again until I had the illusion that I was secure. We'd been warned that fiddling with the tarp was part of the game. Out on a ten-foot ledge for 82 hours with just a sleeping bag, a ground pad, and four gallons of water, I'd fiddle with anything to keep my mind off food!"

On the second day of her solitary sojourn, she wrote, "Last night the moon shone directly into my eyes, not round and friendly but icy cold and distant like a spotlight, silhouetting a rocky moonscape against a charcoal sky. Now at sunrise, my sinuses ache from the cold, and the nearby juniper glistens with incipient frost. There are no profound thoughts, not even a semblance of a vision. It's too cold to think, too cold to pray. The only blessing I long for is a hot cup of tea."

Chances are the vision part of this quest was not a profound glimpse of divine grandeur but rather the dark emptiness at the cold and barren center and the ability to see the cold moon, the glistening juniper. That bleak moment where there was no semblance of a vision *was* the vision at the heart of the quest. Later she recalled, "On that ledge in the Utah desert, that ten-foot expanse of rock that for 82 hours welcomed me and made my home, I called to my awareness all those souls confined to institutional care . . . men and women whose homes have been washed away by flood or tornado or the ravages of war. . . . I held in my heart the children who live under bridges or in cars."

In wilderness there is pain, and in pain there is compassion.

In wilderness there is also beauty and the ability to see it large.

The vision of the quest is in the seeing, inward and outward, that brings the beauty and the pain into one large and intimate picture.

Wilderness vision may actually become more acute in the dark. This darkness is not only the shadows of our own inner psyches but a darkness of cultural context, too. Coming as I do from the enlightenment tradition of liberal religion, I call the power of this darkness "endarkenment." I made up this word when I tried to call the Boston headquarters of the Unitarian Universalist Association. Dialing the wrong area code, I ended up speaking with someone at the Palomar Observatory (the Boston

liberals were apparently only two digits away from heaven). Convinced that there had to be something more to this cosmic slip of the finger than met the eye, I called Palomar again and learned that this observatory, which had been the most significant in the world, was losing its seeing capabilities as a result of "light pollution" from surrounding cities. Were it not for the Native American reservations at the bottom of the mountain inhibiting land development, the observatory's vision would have been impaired even more.

I am intrigued by the notion of another variety of light pollution—a dimming of our inner vision resulting from too much information, too much progress—too much enlightenment, even.

Endarkenment is the wilderness invitation into places holy and strange—places where the light of so-called progress may not have reached. I found myself in such a place when our pilgrim troupe visited the Swayambhunath Monkey Temple complex in Kathmandu, so named for the numerous monkeys that roam the area. We visited on March 12, the day of the Hindu Holi festival, when people paint their faces and throw colored dye at one another. Along the streets, young people dropped water balloons from second- or third-story windows, treating those below to a drenching of festival frolic. In addition to the usual mélange of

Endarkenment is the wilderness invitation into places holy and strange—places where the light of so-called progress may not have reached.

vendors stationed outside the temples were chattering monkeys and painted revelers. Passing through the crowd and inundated with the images of Hindu gods and goddesses carved or painted on temples of every size, several of us entered a Tibetan Buddhist temple, removed our shoes, and stepped respectfully through a passageway illuminated by hundreds of flames flickering in their ritual fashion from brass butter lamps. Inside, it was like another world, where rows of monks bowed repetitiously and chanted their scriptures. We seated ourselves on a mat near the wall. One by one, my Western companions left. I stayed, lulled by the deep, sonorous drone of male voices chanting, the rhythmic cacophony of groaning horns and clanging cymbals, and ceremonial movements or changes of vestments. Without understanding the meaning of their rituals, I seemed to be absorbing the music of the monks into my body.

At some point, I realized that I was not only the only westerner in the room but also the only woman. I had a momentary impulse to flee, as if I were a child suddenly aware of trespassing in a forbidden place. I stayed put, however, and in those moments felt a powerful connection with the monks, who seemed to include me at the same time that they appeared to be oblivious to my presence. Overcoming my discomfort, I allowed mystery and darkness to envelop me. There in that ancient temple, I felt a profound sense of my own place in the human family.

A pilgrim is one who discovers home while not at home, who encounters the familiar in the strange, and whose vision requires darkness. Jerry Godard further underscores the paradox of this encounter in an explication from an essay by Sigmund Freud on the uncanny. Freud's word for uncanny was *unheimlich,* which can also be translated "unhomelike." For Freud, the uncanny is

> that "class of the terrifying which leads us back to something long known to us, once very familiar," arousing a "hidden familiar thing that has undergone repression and has emerged from it suddenly." More horrible than strangeness is the unexpected, unsought presence of the familiar. . . . Freud cleverly demonstrates the etymological equivalence of "otherness" and "familiarity," bridging their difference both psychically and in language. *Unheimlich* and *heimlich* become one: "*Heimlich* (home-like) is a word the meaning of which develops toward an ambivalence until it finally coincides with its opposite, *unheimlich*."[7]

Wilderness is where we meet ourselves. The irony is that we meet our familiar self in the unfamiliar. We bring our humanity into that space of strangeness where darkness sometimes gives us the power to see.

Whether we enter the wilderness of our own hearts and minds, a wilderness of the world's dark mystery, or the majestic wilderness of nature, our journey takes us into the center where what is unhomelike becomes homelike. In the strange music of monasteries, in an empty haunted house, on the rocky shore of an island, in the center of a labyrinth—in some unfamiliar and unexpected place—the pilgrim heart finds home.

chapter four

Finding Home in the Body

Here in this body are the sacred rivers: here are the sun
and moon, as well as all the pilgrimage places.
I have not encountered another temple
as blissful as my own body.

—Saraha

B*enjamin was born and spent his early years* in a small university town in Iowa, surrounded by farms. When he was four, he claimed that like many of the people around him, he too owned a farm, although it was only imaginary. From time to time he told his parents what was going on at his farm. One day he said to his mother, "Mom, you know what happened last night? Last night the vet came and you know what he did? He cut a little piece off the hoof of the cow, and now she has a calf." His mother, who had a talent for seizing opportunities when they present themselves, felt that this was the moment to introduce her son to the facts of life. "Benjamin," she said, "that is not the way it happens." And she embarked on a long story about sperm and eggs and fertilization and how the embryo develops in the womb and how the little calf is finally born between the cow's legs. "You see, Benjamin," she said, "that is how it really happens." Whereupon Benjamin looked her straight in the eye and said, "Not on *my* farm."[1]

As human creatures, we live in bodies—

Bodies that are born amid blood and fluid out of other bodies
Bodies that feel sexual passion and sensual pleasure
Bodies that walk and play baseball and sleep
Bodies that get sick or bleed, bodies that heal
Bodies that see the colors of a sunset and listen to Mozart
  and the Beatles
Bodies that taste strawberries and mold clay
Bodies that eat and drink, urinate and defecate
Bodies that smell the ocean and play the piano
Bodies that give birth and change diapers and drive to work
  and cook dinner
Bodies that read and think and feel and play

Bodies that laugh and weep
Bodies that grow and shrink
Bodies that live and age and die

When it comes to some of the things on this list, we are quite comfortable. When it comes to others, we may assert with Benjamin, "Not on *my* farm."

In Western culture, our discomforts with ourselves as physical beings in a physical world are rooted in our religion, particularly in orthodox Christian theology. Margaret Miles, my professor of Christian church history at Harvard, said something once that has stayed with me for twenty years. She said that the history of Christianity was the attempt to bring body and soul back together.

Contemporary pilgrimage also reflects an attempt to join our human purpose with that of our physical world. Pilgrims of past centuries journeyed across vast stretches of difficult terrain, focusing on their sacred destination and often ignoring their ties with the lands they traveled. For pilgrims of the twenty-first century, however, the spiritual journey invites them to bring body and soul together in the context of our physical environment. Becoming comfortable in our bodies is inseparable from becoming at home in nature. Our fears of danger, suffering, and death are bodily fears. Our bodies do not just exist in and relate to nature, they *are* nature.

One of my favorite movies is *The African Queen,* starring Katherine Hepburn as Rose Sayer, the prim, proper, and prudish spinster sister of an English missionary, and Humphrey Bogart as Charlie Allnut, a boozing, cigar-smoking, unshaven, uncouth captain of a supply launch steamer. Set in East Africa during World War I, the film brings these two unlikely companions together after Rose's brother dies as a result of a German attack, and Charlie's boat, the *African Queen,* presents the only means of escape. There is a scene in the film where Charlie awakens, hung over after binging on gin, to discover that Rose, dressed in white and shaded by a black parasol, has just triumphantly poured the last drop of his entire supply of gin over the side of the boat. Although quite distraught at first, he softens toward her and even shaves his scruffy beard. He attempts to enter a conversation, but she ignores him and reads her Bible in stony silence. Finally he screams at her, "And you call yourself a Christian! . . . What ya being so mean for, Miss? A man takes a drop too much once in a while, it's only human nature." She responds (with a manner of speech that only

For pilgrims of the twenty-first century, the inner journey is the continued endeavor to bring body and soul together, to be at home in our bodies and to relate to our physical world as our home.

Katherine Hepburn could intone), "Nature, Mr. Allnut, is what we are put in this world to rise above."

This line perfectly expresses the essence of the philosophical and theological principles that have perpetuated the division of body and soul. Although we often assume that such beliefs are inherent to Christianity, they actually have their roots in Greek thought. The first Christians were Jews, of course, who believed that to be fruitful and multiply was their charge from God. But Greek thought, especially that of the Stoics, described a natural order in which the highest rank belonged to *logos,* the rational part of the self, and the lowest rank was ascribed to the physical world, or matter. In this hierarchy, Aristotle and other Greek philosophers associated women with matter and men with logos.

Taken to extremes, this dualism found expression as what is known as *body hatred.* The body was considered clay and gore, "a filthy bag of excrement and urine."

What came out of this worldview was a model for Christian virtue based not on the old Jewish ideal of being fruitful and multiplying but on the Greek ideal of transcending the baser nature of the body. The object was to rise above one's body and its many perceived weaknesses.

From Saint Augustine in the fifth century, divisions were reinforced. Augustine taught that marriage in the Garden of Eden was an idyllic state where there was no sexual desire connected with procreation. After the fall of Adam and Eve, however, human beings had to struggle to subdue their passion. The body and its needs and passions thus became even more clearly forces to be struggled against, forces that were not part of an ideal human existence. In the Western world, it was not only normal but even a sign of virtue to deny one's body, to see it as foreign and alienated from God. To grow closer to God, people had to rise above their lower nature, a belief that led in later centuries to the ideal of celibacy and the creation of monasteries for men and convents for women.

Martin Luther rejected celibacy in favor of the ideal of family life, but he still promoted the idea that Eve was the source of sin and the passions of the body were still something to contend with. He wrote: "Today after our nature has become corrupted by sin, woman is needed not only to secure increase, but also for companionship and protection. The management of the household must have the ministration of the dear ladies. In addition, and this is lamentable, woman is also necessary as an antidote against sin. And so, in the case of the woman, we must think not only of the managing of the household which she does, but also of the medicine which she is."[2]

Whether or not we, as women and men, Christians and non-Christians, believe in this dualistic system of body and mind, we are left with its legacy: the struggle to get body and soul back

together—to be more at home in our bodies. We live with our own modern version of body hatred. "Accept your face with serious thanks," wrote Carl Sandburg,[3] but most of us do not accept our facial flaws or bodily bulges. Even healthy activities such as weight control and exercise become addictive and obsessive when we fixate on the "unacceptable" nature of our bodies by starving ourselves to conform to unrealistic standards of thinness or taking anabolic steroids to exaggerate muscle size. About the time we finally make friends with our imperfect faces, we develop wrinkles or lose our hair. Even when we approach routines of exercise or diet with more maturity and moderation, the mirror greets us with flabby arms, multiple chins, and cellulite-dimpled thighs. People read books about spirituality while they are recovering from having their breasts enlarged or their fannies firmed or their faces peeled and lifted.

Beyond that, we abuse our bodies and then expect the health care system to compensate for our behavior. If science would just come up with a pill to reduce weight, I would much prefer taking that pill than moderating my appetite for potatoes, pasta, and chocolate éclairs. When my mother became sick with emphysema after smoking all her life, I would have welcomed the administration of a drug that could erase her years of abuse. If there were a fountain of youth, I would eagerly partake of its elixir to reverse the effects of arthritis and return with nimble knees to the tennis court.

The alienation from our bodies has allowed us to abuse them while at the same time supporting an industry of drugs, procedures, and cosmetics to mask or mend what we have neglected, battered, or abused. The toxic impact of these products on our environment as well as on our bodies is a subject too enormous for this book. The point, however, is that the estrangement from our bodies results in our expectation that drugs, doctors, and therapists will heal or enhance our bodies from the outside in. Bodies are still somehow fundamentally foreign; we treat them as though they are flawed, tiresome, inferior vehicles on which we must constantly work. A spiritual approach calls for us to know that we are our bodies and that health and beauty can only be nurtured from the inside out.

This impulse toward bringing body and soul together in order to experience health and befriend our imperfect, aging bodies finds expression in pilgrimage.

This impulse toward bringing body and soul together in order to experience health and befriend our imperfect, aging bodies finds expression in pilgrimage, not only in physical challenges but also in the choice of religious sites, symbols or themes for journey, and contemplation. In addition to seeking out Christian roots in some of the nondualistic outlaw theologies of Western religion, people are turning now also to non-Western sources in an effort to unite body and soul—to Asian, African, or

Native American religions, where attitudes toward our bodies, our aging, and our eventual death are experienced in the context of our place in the larger context of creation, where death is part of life rather than the enemy of life. This is not to say that all humans do not share the instinctive desire to postpone death and relieve suffering; rather, it is to affirm our connection with the great living system in which even death contributes to life. As we are more immersed in the great holy exuberance of creation and fall more in love with life, our pilgrim hearts are called also to make friends with death.

Like other creatures, we have our instinctive fear of death. But we have more. We live each day with the consciousness that we will die and that the people we love will die. Even when we experience a death, however, we are protected from the physicality of it. Our rituals are constructed in ways that help us avoid rather than enter that experience.[4]

On my pilgrimage in Nepal, we visited Pashupatinath, Nepal's most sacred Hindu shrine, where there is a whole complex of temples to the god Shiva along the Bagmati River. This most sacred of rivers is also the most slimy and polluted I have ever seen, and among the smells there is the sweet putrid smell of the bodies that are cremated on platforms called ghats. The Bagmati River flows into the Ganges, and it is believed that a dip in the Bagmati ensures release from the cycle of rebirth.

In rituals similar to those practiced on the Ganges River in India, bodies are wrapped in cloth, laid on a bamboo lifter, and carried by barefoot pallbearers accompanied by male relatives and mourners. The women stay at home to weep. At the cremation ghat, male family members circle the body and perform rites to ensure a smooth transition into the next world. The body is placed on a log pyre, and the mourners, dressed in white, retreat to watch it burn. It takes about two and a half hours. Then a member of the family crushes the skull, and the remains are swept into the Bagmati.

How different this set of rituals is from contemporary mainstream Western practices, particularly in the United States, where, when someone you love dies, you call the professionals.[5] They take care of everything from there. Perhaps they embalm the body, artificially preserving what would naturally decay and return to creation. If you choose burial, chances are you let the funeral directors dress the body. You might view it to say good-bye. At the cemetery, there will be fake grass covering the mound of dirt from the grave, which will not be visible. Dirt is scarce. I know this because when I do graveside services, I have to ask for dirt to put in the grave. I am usually handed a tiny bag of sand—it's cleaner, I suppose. After the ceremony, it is expected that mourners will leave. Professionals will lower and bury the casket later.

It is not our purpose in life to eliminate death. Yes, we strive to maintain life and health in ourselves and in other beings. We strive

to alleviate suffering. But death is part of our purpose. We have a hard time believing this, which is why we in the Western world have allowed our funeral practices to shield us from the reality of death and protect us from our own grief. It is also why we let doctors and hospitals do very expensive things to our bodies and the bodies of those we love even when those bodies are ready to give out.

Death is not just something we cannot avoid; it is part of a cosmic or divine purpose, and the better we are able to understand that, the more at home we will be in our mortal bodies. As physician Lewis Thomas writes, "We will have to give up the notion that death is catastrophe, or detestable, or avoidable, or even strange. We will need to learn more about the cycling of life in the rest of the system, and about our connection to the process."[6]

Death is not just something we cannot avoid; it is part of the cosmic or divine purpose, and the better we are able to understand that, the more at home we are in our mortal bodies.

The pilgrim heart makes friends with death because death is part of life—and part of the life's journey.

I was deeply moved by a story I heard Wendy Johnson tell at a conference on Zen meditation and writing that she led with Natalie Goldberg. Wendy is a lay Zen priest, and for many years she was the head gardener at Green Gulch Farm in Marin County, California, just north of San Francisco.

Early one morning, the rainbow lettuce at Green Gulch had lured a deer into the vegetable garden. The gardeners approached on their morning errands and frightened the deer. Instinctively, it bolted, running into a fence and breaking its neck. But it was still alive. The anguished gardeners went to their master. "What shall we do?" they asked. "Should we kill it?" Their teacher said, "Stay with it. Sit with it." So they sat with the deer as its life ebbed, blood gurgling from its limp neck. Then they made a cradle in the compost pile, placed the deer on the pile, and covered it with alfalfa, hay, and garbage. Months later, when they dug into the compost pile, only the hooves were left.

Wendy ended this story with a question: "How did we get so tame?"

How did we get so tame? Part of how we got so tame took hundreds of years, as we became less and less at home in our bodies and less at home in the great living system—a system where the insect eats the leaf and the frog eats the insect and the snake eats the frog and so on. In talking about having a soul that persists into eternity, we must not forget that we humans are not the only ones who live and die. The best thing we can do for our souls is to get acquainted with the whole living system of which we are a part.

Our world is not a fallen paradise where we need to rise above our nature; it is a blessed garden where we are called to "sit" with our human and nonhuman companions through their suffering—

a garden where new life comes out of death. Among the images from trekking in Nepal that has stayed with me is that of a large family, including children of various ages, sitting with a dying cow, just sitting with it, silent and together. The cow is sacred in Hindu culture—not loved as a pet or just valued for its usefulness but revered as a sacred gift of creation. Like the Buddhists who expressed their compassion toward the deer by suffering with it instead of hastening its death or avoiding its presence, the people of this family took time out from their daily chores to offer compassion to the cow. Many humans in Western culture do not receive this kind of loving attention.

> *If life and the soul are sacred, the human body is sacred.*
>
> —Walt Whitman, *Song of Myself*

Yes, I ask with Wendy Johnson, "How did we get so tame?" Our pilgrim task is to claim our bodily identification with our natural world and to become more at home in this house of flesh and bone, water and air—more at home with our sensual, sexual, physically flawed, and mortal selves.

The impulse for wholeness is not only in relationship to one's body, however, but in relationship to the world of matter. The same beliefs that have divided us from our physical nature have also divided us from the physical world, where we humans have exploited and endangered our fragile and beautiful earth. Beginning with Rachel Carson's classic revelation of our human plague on the planet in *The Silent Spring*, we have been educated through decades of evidence of environmental apocalypse. Most of the green prophets appeal to us to change our behavior on behalf of our desire to avoid extinction. "This is our home," they are saying; "let's take care of it so it will be here for future generations."

This is a worthy admonition. The message, however, does not really hit home, so to speak, because the prevailing ethos is that the earth and all its creatures function on behalf of human beings. The Book of Genesis (1:26–28) tells us that Adam named the plants and the animals and was given "dominion over the fish of the sea, and over the birds of the air, and over the cattle, and over all the earth, and over every creeping thing." God charged Adam and Eve to "be fruitful and multiply, and fill the earth and subdue it." As long as humans justify this exploitive relationship with creation, we will not change our ways.

The modern-day pilgrim has an opportunity to travel a very different path from the pilgrims of previous ages. In former times, and perhaps in many current pilgrimage traditions, pilgrims have sought to *rise above* their physical nature in order to live a more pure and holy existence. Spirituality meant being in but not of the

world. Not only did human beings receive divine sanction for pillaging the earth, but also the human soul would transcend this physical world to dwell with God in heaven. The subtle and unconscious assumption underlying this belief was that the welfare of the earth was of little consequence.

Pilgrims of the twenty-first century need a context for getting body and soul into a harmonious relationship with one another *and* with their physical surroundings in order to live the pure and holy life of their aspirations. It is not enough to want to preserve our planet for our sake. We have to want to preserve it for *its own* sake, because it too is a divine creation.

I am among many contemporary pilgrims who have found their way to sites in Ireland and Scotland where the Druids and Christians of Celtic tradition have left a sacred imprint on the landscape. Celtic tradition is not at odds with the body and its natural environment. Pelagius, a Celtic Christian who was born the same year as Augustine and clashed with him, was condemned for pantheism—for identifying the divinity in all of creation. He did not believe that the flesh was corrupt. He believed that women were equal to men. For these beliefs, however, he was excommunicated. Celtic Christianity, called "the contrary way," was suppressed for hundred of years but has been revived in more recent decades by Christians who find meaning in their creation-centered approach.

For the Celtic Christians, divine energy came in feminine as well as masculine forms, and women enjoyed equal social status. There were priests and priestesses, abbots and abbesses—with equal education and authority. Their monasteries were more university than cloister, and the only reason to go in was to come back out with something to offer the world. This was in contrast to the monasteries and convents where men and women could avoid temptation or rise above their nature by separating themselves from the world.

The Celtic Christians' heresy, pantheism, was a belief that divine holy spirit dwells in all of creation, including the fish of the sea, the birds of the air, the cattle, and every creeping thing. The "soul" was not the exclusive province of human beings; it was the spark of divine energy in all life. Celtic legends are filled with fish, otters, and birds that have souls. One saint is said to have had a horse who wept when the saint died.[7] (In contrast, I have a software program that alerts me to the fact that *who* is not a proper pronoun for referring to a horse.) Celtic blessings, like Native American prayers, reflect a theology where humans are neither stewards nor exploiters of creation. We are just part of it and charged to be mindful of how our part affects the whole. If the salmon don't run or the cows don't give milk or the hummingbirds don't return in the spring, we must consider how our daily routines have disrupted the fragile balance of life. Our role is to

make our home in that context, ever conscious that nature is not ours to subdue or dominate because it is not ours, period.

I went to the Celtic island of Iona because I knew it would be a place where the holy would touch me, all of me, through the senses. I also knew that it is possible to connect in spiritually powerful ways when we are not rising above our physical nature—when we are in touch with ourselves as passionate, sensual, and mortal beings. The more we are in touch with our bodies, the more we are in touch with creation. And the more we are in touch with creation, the more we live in harmony with it. When we are in harmony with creation and with our own bodies as part of it, we are more alive—and more at home.

On my last afternoon on Iona, I wanted to revisit several significant places and explore new ones. There was not time, however, and I felt myself becoming anxious as I considered how to spend these last precious hours. I realized that I could try to get to several places and end up so worried about doing it all that I would not be truly present anywhere, so I decided to set out toward the north beach with no further itinerary and let the island speak to me. It was a clear day, perhaps the first such day of that week. The sun of early spring streaked a brisk chilly wind with balmy gusts. My path took me through several small crofts (farms), where sheep and lambs were accustomed to pilgrim invasions. If I approached the animals, however, they bolted from their leisurely grazing and scurried to a comfortable distance before resuming their repast. I was careful to close gates as I traversed private property on the island, where the well-worn paths of sheep and pilgrims signaled the common understanding that private ownership of land does not preclude public use of it. Coming from a country where walking through someone else's property is called trespassing and where people arm themselves with guns in readiness to defend their rights of ownership, I enjoyed a hospitality of the land that seems to prevail throughout much of Europe. The invitation to public access invites a spirit of respectfulness toward both the land and its stewards, with an unspoken sense of participation in the kind of community that nurtures neighborly generosity.

I was drawn to the north end of the island, where white beaches and clear waters as blue as the Caribbean merged with rocky shores reminiscent of the Northern California coast. Finding a sheltered cove with exposure to the sun, I lay down on my back directly on the warm sand, arms outstretched. I was aware of what a vulnerable posture this was and grateful for these moments when I felt embraced in a world that was beautiful and good. I must have slipped into a light sleep, for I was startled by a nudge on my leg. I raised my head and found myself face to face with a sheep and two lambs. We shared a brief moment of mutual astonishment before they scrambled over a dune and out of sight.

The sheep, so commonplace on the island, were certainly not wild animals, but that moment when one of them nudged me—that moment of touching that was initiated by the sheep and not by me—felt like a gift of wildness. It may be a gift that is available more than I know, but most of the time I am not in a posture for receiving it. Even in the wilderness of Alaska, where I witnessed bears a few yards away devouring spawning salmon or encountered elk lounging in our campground, I was the sightseer, not the companion. I related to the creatures of the wild with binoculars or camera, as if I could tame them with lens and shutter.

When I was a child living near the ocean, I enjoyed exploring the rocks at low tide, where, in addition to counting the starfish, I sought out the round, colorful sea anemones. I would poke my finger into the middle of the sea anemones so I could feel them close around it and "hug" it. It did not occur to me that this was not a pleasant activity for the anemone. Later, of course, I realized that this creature was not hugging my finger; it was responding to an enemy invasion. As an adult, however, I also see that I have lost something of the child's trusting relationship. I want to be able to retrieve the child's intimacy with wildness at the same time that I see the importance of honoring the fears and needs of other beings.

Pilgrimages real or metaphorical invite us into a posture that is receptive to the gift of wildness, engaging it rather than witnessing or observing it. What this means, I do not really know. For someone who hunts or angles for food, it means thinking like the animal or fish and stalking it; then killing it, gutting it, and preparing it for eating. For someone who farms or gardens, it means partnering with creation to produce a harvest. For a biologist or naturalist, it means exploring habitats and habits, perhaps using scientific knowledge to benefit human community. For a mystic, it means just being in and part of the wild. The hunter with a pilgrim heart, however, feels respect and compassion for his prey, and does not kill wastefully or take pleasure in killing. The farmer with a pilgrim heart replenishes the soil that feeds her and does not poison the air. The scientist with a pilgrim heart holds sacred the welfare of the subjects of an experiment. The mystic with a pilgrim heart cares for the future that is someone else's present.

Pilgrimages real or metaphorical invite us into a posture that is receptive to the gift of wildness, engaging it rather than witnessing or observing it.

We who live in a culture with an infrastructure built on the practice of exploitation need to create pilgrim opportunities for ourselves and others—experiences where we *feel* our kinship with the fish of the sea and the birds of the air and the cattle of the fields and every creeping thing. Naturalist and explorer John Muir

offered a model for exploration when he talked about his "method of study":

> I drifted about from rock to rock, from stream to stream. Where night found me, there I camped. When I discovered a new plant, I sat down beside it, for a minute or a day, to make its acquaintance and try to hear what it had to say. When I came to moraines or ice scratches upon the rocks, I traced them, learning what I could of the glaciers that made them. I asked the boulders I met whence they came and whither they were going.[8]

Muir's intimacy with the souls of plants and stones as well as the creatures of the wild is reminiscent of Thoreau, whose Walden Pond pilgrimage near Concord, Massachusetts, was an intimate exploration of sacred landscape. Today Walden Pond is a pilgrim site, a place where people brave the summer traffic or charter tour buses to visit landscape made holy by one man's record of doing trade with "the Celestial Empire." Placing another rock on the cairn of devotion in a place now tamed with the commercial enterprises that Thoreau abjured, their hearts sip the metaphorical tonic of wildness.

Sacred landscape—wild or tamed—offers the tonic of wildness because it invites us into a relationship of kinship and trust with the natural world and stirs a deeper consciousness of our place in it.

❧

One of our spiritual practices on the pilgrimage in Nepal was "conscious eating," the discipline of maintaining silence during the first course of our evening meal, which was generally homemade soup. This provided an opportunity to reflect on the sources of our nourishment and to be present in the sensory experience of the meal. Not only were we made more aware of the porters who carried our food on their backs and the cooks and Sherpas who prepared and served our meals, but we felt a kinship with the land and the people who farmed it. We made the connection between the cow manure that children gathered from the path and the fuel that warmed some of the food set before us. Fellow pilgrim Jerry Engelhardt writes of the practice of conscious eating:

> Typically my reflection would start with the soil and the small, irregularly shaped terraces that had been so laboriously formed out of the steep Himalayan mountainsides on which the potatoes, beans, rice, or other vegetables in our soup had been grown. As we trekked, we had witnessed the hard manual labor of the local Nepalese people as they hand-cleared the rocks and weeds from small plots of

> ground, utilizing primitive plows pulled by oxen or yak-type animals. I would think about how hard they worked and how they probably worried if their crops would get enough rain and sunshine to grow so that they could feed their families and perhaps have enough left to sell a small portion. . . . Then thinking of God's gift of rain, sunshine, and the miracle of a small seed growing into beautiful life-sustaining plants, I would visualize the growth of the plants, the weeding of the small plots of land by hand, the irrigation process of channeling the rain to migrate from one terrace level down to another on the steep mountain-side, and finally the harvest. In addition to the farmers, I would think of the other people who were involved in the process of buying, selling, and finally preparing the food for our use. Set before us, then, was this wonderfully tasty soup, elegantly beautiful in its simplicity, ready for our consumption, and often richly garnished by popcorn sprinkled over the top as a final presentation.

Although our porters carried items such as rice, tea, and canned fruit from the city (in addition to all the utensils, dishes, and supplies needed for food preparation), we became conscious of how local villagers contributed to our fare. I recall walking through the village of Tatopani, for example, and noticing a small shop where shelves were stacked with caged chickens. I predicted to my walking companion that we would be treated to very fresh chicken for dinner. Indeed, fried chicken was on the menu that evening.

The practice of conscious eating deepens gratitude. For those of us who eat the flesh of other creatures, it sharpens our awareness of what it is that we do when we participate in the death of another life in order to smell, taste, chew, and swallow the substance of their bodies into our bodies. For those who do not eat fish, fowl, or meat, a daily decision is made to spurn their carnivorous nature. What distinguishes a spiritual approach to eating is not just what we eat but how our eating reflects our kinship with nature and our recognition that other creatures are our brothers and sisters. They nurture their young and grieve the deaths of their companions. They bask in the sun, romp in the grass, and bleed. We mustn't forget, we are animals, too.

What distinguishes a spiritual approach to eating is not just what we eat but how our eating reflects our kinship with nature and our recognition that other creatures are our brothers and sisters.

In the ancient worldview of the Celts, people knew without having to philosophize, theologize, or theorize that before you are free to wander safely, you must first have roots; you have to know the earth, and some place on it, as home. And you have to know it

in your body as well as your soul. The Celtic knot that decorates borders with patterns of graceful and intricate simplicity, often depicting animal scenes, offers a symbolic reminder that "the great chain of being stretches back beyond humanity. When human memory runs out, you can draw on the deeper songs of animals and rocks and trees."[9] Woven through this continuous chain is the Holy—the presence that inspires and breathes and motivates all things. This pulsing chain is our home, and we are not only *in* it, we are *of* it, and it is of us.

chapter five

With Strangers and Others

We touch this strength, our power, who we are in the world, when we are most fully in touch with one another and with the world.

—Carter Heyward

S*tar Island, a rocky mound* that is part of a cluster of islands ten miles off the U.S. coast of New Hampshire and Maine, is a pilgrimage destination for many who journey there for a week or two in summer. More than a summer camp for people of all ages or a conference center devoted to learning, religious values, and creativity, Star Island is a spiritual preserve. When you board the boat for the hour's ride to the island, you enter a world without cars, without telephones, without television. Until the 1950s, communication with the mainland was via carrier pigeon. Your drinking water comes on the boat with you; you will get two showers during your week's stay if the cistern has been blessed with rain; and the sea offers a generous supply of water for flushing toilets. You will fill a pitcher with hot water from a central supply and take it to your room to bathe, using the pitcher and bowl provided there. You will receive a pitcher of drinking water for brushing your teeth. During your first evening on the island, you will hear the traditional "fire and water talk," during which you are encouraged to conserve water and warned that to smoke or otherwise allow an open flame in the island's historic New England clapboard buildings is an offense that will result in your immediate banishment.

Although there are diverse themes for the weekly conferences, you can count on having the opportunity to participate in the rituals that take place throughout the summer. An early morning bell announces the polar bear swim at seven (a ritual in which I have never indulged), and a singing troupe awakens conferees with familiar tunes adapted to provide an appetizing preview of the breakfast menu. Weekly evening options include a talent show, a bonfire, and a lobster dinner. The college-age young people who staff the island are called Pelicans. Keepers of the rituals, most of them have been coming to Star Island with their parents or

grandparents since they were very young. Some of them will hold their weddings on the island; some will return with their children and grandchildren; some will ask to have their ashes scattered in Gosport Harbor, on East Rock, or in that sacred place where they return each year for their morning meditations.

Every night at about nine, participants in the conference gather on the porch of the old hotel in preparation for the evening service, held in the small stone chapel on a rocky knoll at the island's highest point. If you wish to attend evening chapel services, you line up on the porch and chatter while you wait for the procession to the chapel to begin. Conversation ceases abruptly when the signal is given, and you move slowly and silently, two by two, up the path. As you step onto the path, about half of you receive a candle lantern, which you will carry to light your way and then hang on a wall bracket for the candlelight service. It is like a mini-pilgrimage as silence and candlelight mark a time and space apart.

Conversation ceases abruptly when the signal is given, and you move slowly and silently, two by two, up the path. As you step onto the path, about half of you receive a candle lantern, which you will carry to light your way and then hang on a wall bracket for the candlelight service. It is like a mini-pilgrimage as silence and candlelight mark a time and space apart.

On my first visit to Star Island, something extraordinary happened one evening during the procession to evening chapel. As we walked up the footpath in silence, the only sounds those of feet on gravel and the clinking of the glass chimneys in their metal holders, the entire procession became wordlessly aware of an umbrella of light directly over the chapel, shimmering in streaks of brightness and color that appeared to pour down the inside of a giant cosmic bowl.

We entered the chapel reluctantly, but our corporate awe was palpable, and we carried it through the service and back out into the night, where the sky still danced with light. Several of us then congregated outside to enjoy this unusual migration of the aurora borealis into the skies of southern Maine. Lying on the ground, we rested our heads on each other's stomachs, creating a crisscross herringbone pattern of human pillows.

Each of us might have taken in the gift of that night alone, and it would have been special. But because we were there, in a context of sacred space together, there was another dimension to the experience. Social anthropologist Victor Turner calls this dimension *communitas.*

Communitas *is what happens when a whole group of people cross a threshold and together enter liminal time and space—that is, an in-between time that is neither past nor present and a space that is neither here nor there.*

Communitas is what happens when a whole group of people cross a threshold and together enter liminal time and space—

that is, an in-between time that is neither past nor present and a space that is neither here nor there. In that threshold space, they experience a bond, and it is not like any bond they may experience in their ordinary, structured lives.[1] It is not the same as community, which we may cultivate in our churches or clubs or even our neighborhoods, mostly with people who are like us in terms of social or economic status. In *communitas,* people experience a comradeship "in and out of time" that reveals, however fleetingly, some recognition of a larger social bond. In *communitas,* there are no social roles, status, or hierarchical structures. Everyone is equal. Even more significant, everyone *feels* what it is to be equal and feels the potential for who we can be as a human family.

In *communitas,* there is a dimension of ecstatic experience—ecstatic in the sense of religious ecstasy, which is the experience of being outside oneself, transcending the usual structures of ordinary life. I felt that ecstasy when I shared the experience of the northern lights with others on Star Island. First, our candlelight procession was not just a string of individuals; it was a group—a larger entity. Later, our chain of human beings with heads resting on one another's stomachs linked

> *A human life is like a single letter in the alphabet. It can be meaningless. Or it can be part of a great meaning.*
>
> —Jewish Theological Seminary of America

us all in that cosmic dimension that embraced us so fully. We were oblivious to whether a politically liberal head rested on a conservative stomach or vice versa.

This experience in isolation could have been nothing more than a drug-free high. What made it more was the context of our being there on a pilgrimage of sorts, where our intention was to be touched by the holy in ways that enhance our sense of connection with the great human family. And that is really what *communitas* is about.

It is important to remind ourselves of the joys and depths of *communitas* in this age of spiritual quests that often seem to be more about "me" than about "us." If a mystical experience is grounded in the truly spiritual, it will connect us with the fundamental source of truth. William James, in his classic book *The Varieties of Religious Experience,* sought to get beyond the pathological dimensions of mystical experiences and describe what is common to all religions. He came up with four major characteristics:

> It is ineffable. You cannot describe it in words. It has to be experienced first hand.
>
> You receive some kind of insight or illumination of the depths of truth.
>
> It is transient. It cannot be sustained for more than a brief time.

> You are passive. You might do something like meditate or fast to induce a mystical consciousness, but your experience is one of being grasped by a superior power.[2]

If a mystical experience is also religious, you feel a connection with the transcendent—with the divine or holy Spirit as you understand it. You transcend your earthly limitations and are part of something much greater. You lose yourself in it and feel your sense of belonging to the whole. You belong to more than yourself and more than your family or loved ones. You belong to it all, and in that belonging you feel what it means to be at home.

James pointed out that the common element in such experiences is a "cosmic consciousness." The chief characteristic of a cosmic consciousness is an awareness of the life and order of the universe. Along with this consciousness, there is an intellectual enlightenment and a state of moral exaltation—an indescribable feeling of elevation, elation, and joyousness, and a quickening of the moral sense. With these comes what may be called a sense of immortality, a consciousness of eternal life. This is not a conviction that you *will* have eternal life but a consciousness that you *have it already.*[3]

I think there is a direct connection between the intimations of immortality that we receive via our cosmic consciousness and the way we live in relationship to the people and other beings in our environment. The experience of *communitas* gives us a glimpse of what is possible among us.

In the early 1980s, I ran in a race called the Bonne Belle (named for its sponsor), and I had a surprising and empowering experience that gave me this kind of glimpse. It was all women running—six thousand women—through the streets of Boston.

We took our positions for the race. Jammed together like cattle in claustrophobic readiness, we waited for the signal to begin. Even after the signal was given, and all six thousand of us let out a unison cheer, we still waited for the wall of runners ahead of us to pour into the stream of the race. When I got to the starting line, the thinning wall of runners became a rumbling herd, and I could finally see the crowds who lined the street on either side. Men, women, children. Strangers, friends. They were there to cheer the winners, and we were all winners. They were there cheering for women, not just women who run, but all women who live in a world in which most of the races are run by men and won by men.

I felt something I had never experienced so powerfully before. It was the positive power of groupthink. We know there is a negative power of groupthink, as in Hitler's Germany or in cults like the Jim Jones cult in Guyana. But this was groupthink working on behalf of the holy. This was *communitas.*

There was a power in being part of the pack. Never particularly militant in my feminism, I felt a deep sense of pride and empowerment. I felt a closer identification with the women of history whose bonds have deepened with their common resolve to be treated with respect and dignity. Even as I passed other runners, or when faster competitors overtook me, there was camaraderie among us. Buoyed by the spirit of unity, I forgot that I was even in a race.

At about the five-mile mark, I became aware of a pain in my side, and I had to slow to a walk. I didn't think I would finish the race. But then I turned a corner rimmed with spectators and heard someone on the sidewalk say, "Relax a few minutes! You'll get there!" He was right. Soon I was running again. As I crossed the finish line, I did not want to see my time, for I had lost at least two or three minutes, to be sure. It was a few weeks later that the time came in the mail: I had run faster in that race than any time before or since.

Religious ecstasy is a time when you are outside of yourself; you feel a kind of anonymity, a oneness with nature and with other human beings.

This experience, like our human chain of sky-gazers on Star Island, was ecstatic. Religious ecstasy is a time when you are outside of yourself; you feel a kind of anonymity, a oneness with nature and with other human beings. I have read that a common element in experiences like this one is also a sense of equality among people that transcends normal social barriers. For a few moments you are part of something much larger and more powerful than yourself.

In the 1970s, a friend of mine marched in a protest demonstration against the racist activities of the Ku Klux Klan in Greensboro, North Carolina. She describes the experience of reaching a hilltop. Looking in both directions down the hill, she saw people as far as she could see—thousands of them moving along like one great organism. It was an epiphany of *communitas.*

This bonding is the power of people coming together to celebrate a purpose larger than themselves. Such experiences of bonding and purpose connect people of all ages and cultural backgrounds. I have experienced the same kind of ecstasy and bonding in large demonstrations for peace or human rights.

Sometimes *communitas* happens in situations where people come together not voluntarily but because they are pulled together by events out of their control. Think of the experience of being in something like a blizzard or an earthquake or a hurricane. During a blizzard that brought four-foot drifts of snow up to my door, I got to know neighbors I had never even spoken with before, and some of us hiked to the store to get supplies for others less able to make the walk. I have also lived in the path of more than one hurricane over the years. What I remember more than all

the hours of cleanup and repair is the time when we had a neighborhood cookout after about a week without water or electricity. Take away a few of our basic human comforts, and we are invited to shed some of the personal veneer as well. When we can't get to school or work or all those important scheduled meetings because the roads are blocked with trees or snow, and we can't watch television or listen to music; and when we can't even clean our bodies or flush a toilet without importing our water supply, we have things in common with the people next door and things to laugh about with the folks across the street. A disaster—an extraordinary event such as a big storm—invites us to share our physical possessions and our personal lives. It invites us to notice one another, which we don't do most of the time.

The spirit of pilgrimage comes home in times when extraordinary events interrupt the structures of everyday, thus creating the conditions for being touched by the holy. You do not have to travel to experience the power of *communitas,* but you do need to be in a context outside the structure of everyday life. You need to be open to the experience where the barriers that separate you from others can be removed. Perhaps hardest of all, you need to be willing, as a unique individual, to be lost in a larger identity.

Since the removal of the structures and barriers that bind us to our routine existence is part of a pilgrimage experience, the pilgrim heart is a heart more open than others to the power of *communitas.*

I believe that the ecstasy that I felt in the Bonne Belle race and that my friend felt in the Greensboro demonstration and that all of us feel from time to time when we have an extraordinary experience of bonding with our fellow human beings is a sign of the spiritual power available to us when we are able to participate in a vision that is larger and deeper than our own individual lives. We actually experience ourselves as if we are part of a larger identity. This involves both a consciousness of our individual part and a sense of being lost in the whole organism.

Physician Lewis Thomas argues convincingly that the physical world operates from a larger purpose that requires us to function as if we were all part of one organism. I particularly like his description of how a community of termites functions.

He begins by describing a one-celled protozoan that lives in the digestive tract of Australian termites. This creature produces the enzymes that break down cellulose into carbohydrate, leaving only a nondegradable product the termite excretes in geometrically tidy pellets and then uses as building blocks for erecting vaults and arches for its nest. The protozoan inside the termite appears to have flagella, but they are actually spirochetes that have attached themselves at regular intervals all over the surface of the protozoan. Then, attached to the spirochetes are bacteria that probably help produce the enzymes that break down the cellulose.

Anyway, two or three termites will begin to pick up pellets and move them from place to place, but nothing comes of it. Then more join in, and they seem to reach a critical mass. They place pellets atop pellets, building up columns and beautiful curving, symmetrical arches, and creating the crystalline architecture of vaulted chambers. It isn't known how they communicate with each other, how the chains of termites building one column know when to turn toward the crew on the adjacent column, or how, when the time comes, they manage the flawless joining of the arches.

All of this termite community work could be going on in the walls of your home or office. In fact, there is a whole ecosystem of interdependent cooperative relationships inside every termite that is munching away in homes throughout the world. The termites operate with amazing cooperation toward a common goal.[4]

This is just one little example, but it helps illustrate how intricate, subtle, and sublime the world around us is. Each cell in your body and mine is a walking ecosystem as complex as Jamaica Bay, and each one of those cells is "smarter" than we are.[5] So much for the hubris of human dominion!

I am not a scientist, but I know enough to feel that there is a biological basis for religious or spiritual experience. That does not decrease my sense of reverence or awe; it increases it. I affirm my place in an incredibly complex and interdependent network of relationships. The more I consider the miracle of the termite community, the more I feel there is a purpose that is inscribed in the DNA of every living cell as well as in every moving molecule of the piece of wood being converted to termite nests.

Lewis Thomas also presents a good argument from science to support the notion that living beings, including humans, are genetically programmed to look after one another. After observing that birds, baboons, zebras, wildebeests, and wild dogs will risk their own lives for the sake of the flock or the herd, he states:

> I have no difficulty in imagining a close enough resemblance among the genomes of all human beings, of all races and geographic origins, to warrant a biological mandate for all of us to do whatever we can to keep the rest of us, the species, alive. I maintain, despite the moment's evidence against the claim, that we are born and grow up with a fondness for each other, and we have genes for that. We can be talked out of it, for the genetic message is like a distant music and some of us are hard-of-hearing. Societies are noisy affairs, drowning out the sound of ourselves and our connection. Hard-of-hearing, we go to war. Stone-deaf, we make thermonuclear missiles. Nonetheless, the music is there, waiting for more listeners.[6]

Communitas is what happens when we hear the distant music Lewis Thomas talks about—the music from the soul's true home, the music of our human purpose, a purpose programmed into our DNA even. Such moments are intimations of a unity and harmony that offers hope for our survival as a species. They are peak experiences that cannot be sustained but are sustaining in the hope they offer for what is possible among people. They point to a larger truth that says that in spite of our differences, we share something of the Spirit with each other. We know it in our souls because once in a while it overwhelms us with a sense of communion or connection. Once we participate in such a vision of connection, we may go for weeks or months or years before it happens again. Like any religious experience, we may even dismiss it as a moment of emotional power that carried us away and has no meaning beyond just that.

If it is truly a religious experience, however, it will withstand the test of "So what?" This is the term I use for measuring whether or not an experience is truly spiritual. You can feel elated and even connected as a result of an ecstatic experience, but if there is not a revelation in that context that translates into a life-giving way of engaging with life, the experience is not religious. It is nothing more than an emotional high, and it may as well be something you could induce with drugs.

Too much of what is called spiritual these days is more emotional than spiritual, more self-centered than self-centering, more about spirits beyond us than spirits among us. As I define it, spirituality is gratitude, reverence, and compassion nurtured in the service of love, justice, and hope. If an experience meets the test of "So what?" it operates in the service of love, justice, and hope.

I believe it is something more than a spiritual high, this ecstasy of communion. It is fuel for the work we have to do when we get back home from our real and metaphorical pilgrimages and return to the everyday matters of living together. It is a powerful reminder that our purpose in this life is to join with the Spirit of creation. It is our genes speaking to us, saying *do not go to war, do not destroy the ozone layer, do not poison the air and foul the water.*

Spirituality is gratitude, reverence, and compassion nurtured in the service of love, justice, and hope. If an experience meets the test of "So what?" it operates in the service of love, justice, and hope.

It also offers something like intimations of immortality. If you lose yourself in a sense of the whole, even in a brief ecstatic experience, you receive a sense of being part of the Big Plan and more at home in the world. That doesn't mean you know what the plan is or just how you fit in. Maybe you don't have to know. It does not mean you know what kind of deity or creative force might be driving the Big Plan. It just means you have a sense of knowing, and it helps—especially on those days when you read the news and it appears that things are going amok.

A couple of years ago, in Edward O. Wilson's best-selling book *Consilience,* I learned the meaning of the word he made his title. Consilience just means that moral reasoning and the natural sciences are quite compatible.[7] Lewis Thomas said the same thing thirty years ago. What it all boils down to is that there is plenty of evidence in biology for establishing moral codes of cooperation and community.

It is a curious thing that science in the third millennium is affirming the kind of connections with creation that are part of ancient religions, Celtic Christian tradition, and Native American religion. It doesn't really matter whether you believe there are natural or supernatural forces at work because the sophisticated scientist and the faithful mystic can arrive at the same place, sharing a common sense of reverence and connection, a common sense of relationship, a common bonding in communion, a common identification with a moral code that maintains the balance in it all.

The intellect (what we might call our "pilgrim head") knows that the power of *communitas* offers a glimpse of the possibility for genuine community and solidarity among the citizens, human and nonhuman, of Planet Earth. But the pilgrim heart embraces that knowing as holy and senses that the soul's journey home follows a path of purposeful community.

The reality of translating the experience of *communitas* into the interactions of everyday life once you are back in ordinary space and time is another matter. Witness what happened to Malcolm X, Black Muslim leader in the 1960s, after he returned from the Islamic *hajj,* where he had experienced a feeling of solidarity with people who were different from him but who shared his faith. He described his pilgrimage experience:

> Love, humility, and true brotherhood was almost a physical feeling wherever I turned. . . . All ate as One. . . and slept as One. Everything about the pilgrimage atmosphere accented the Oneness of Man under One God. . . . Never have I witnessed such sincere hospitality and the overwhelming spirit of true brotherhood as is practiced by people of all colors and races, here in this Ancient, Holy Land.[8]

Inspired by his experience of *communitas,* Malcolm X returned home from the Muslim pilgrimage with zeal for changing his approach in order to work for a new vision of "true brotherhood." But he was assassinated by people in his organization whose structures of meaning and relating were threatened by his message.

Even for those who feel the power of *communitas* while on pilgrimage, the experience is not easy to put into practice once they return to life as usual. For example, a Hindu woman of the higher Brahmin caste became friends with women of lower caste while

they were on pilgrimage together. When the lower-caste women expressed a desire to come to visit her in her home, one of them asked, "But will you behave with us then as you are behaving now?" The Brahmin wrote, "It was a simple question, but it touched me to the quick. We have been living near each other for thousands of years, but they are still not of us, and we are not of them."[9]

This brings up the issue of what happens when the sense of being at home in sacred time and sacred space clashes with the structures of the home we have in ordinary time. As Malcolm X's fate illustrates, spiritual transformation can be costly. But how spiritually costly was it for the Brahmin woman to return from her journey and go back to treating the lower-caste women as if they were inferior?

Most of us do not have to deal with such dramatic clashes. If you have felt the power of a peak experience, however, you are transformed, and it will probably mean confronting some changes. To be at home in your sense of belonging with holy purpose is, perhaps by definition, to be at odds with the structures of human community in your world-home.

The Reverend Martin Luther King Jr. is reputed to have said, "There are some things in our world to which persons of goodwill must be maladjusted. Human salvation lies in the hands of the creatively maladjusted." Indeed, our restlessness may lead to creative maladjustment in a world where racial, cultural, or economic inequities thwart the spiritual destiny of our human community.

The pilgrim heart seeks a peacefulness of belonging that is also a restlessness. It may feel anything but peaceful. The paradox is that there is no soul-peace that is not also unrest; there is no family that does not include strangers; there is no true home that is not a world-home.

chapter six

Returning Home

We must be still and still moving
Into another intensity
For a further union, a deeper communion
Through the dark cold and the empty desolation,
The wave cry, the wind cry, the vast waters
Of the petrel and porpoise. In my end is my beginning.

—T. S. Eliot, "East Coker"

A turtle, it is said, carries its home on its back. Observing life in the pond near my home, I know that is not true, at least not for the snapping turtles that crowd this pond and others in the region. Neighbors tell me that you can trap the turtles and transport them several miles away to another pond or creek, and they will find their way back, over land, to their home pond.

It is a mystery, this inner drive, this cosmic compass that guides the turtles of Moores Pond or the swallows of Capistrano or the geese and swans of Chesapeake Bay. In spring, when the mallards and wood ducks land on the pond, I wonder, "Have they been here before? Are these the ducklings that hatched last year? Is the male wood duck showing off his home pond to his new companion? Is this home to them?"

And how about us humans? Do we have an inner affinity for a particular home environment? Most of us, it seems, are drawn to the sea or the desert, the plains or the mountains, the forests or the lakes. What is it in the human psyche that craves foliage or snow or water or sand? Does it have to do with where we were born or grew up, or are there other inner drives and instincts that determine our attractions? Some scientists say that every vertebrate has a genetically transmitted habitat preference.[1] So maybe it is in our DNA—the urge to dwell in the trees or on a hill or next to water or near the ocean or in the middle of a field. Even those whose souls are nourished by living in the city are drawn to a city near water or in the desert or at the foot of a mountain range. I don't mean that we all *live* in the landscape that draws us. Many of us, in fact, may create our homes in a place that is quite the opposite of whatever attracts us. But there is still something in our genes that wants to go where the landscape feeds our spirit.

Pilgrimage takes us into what I call "homescapes," places where we feel an inner rootedness, where we know intuitively that even if we are in a strange, wild, and faraway place, we are home. Such places deepen our sense of belonging in creation and invite us into the wilderness of our own hearts, where we are more open to spiritual transformation. There is an element of being *called* into a pilgrim space where we meet the home of our heart and bring it back to the home of our lives.

When our group of thirteen pilgrims first gathered on the eve of our departure for Thailand and Nepal, we were asked to tell the group why we had come. "The mountains are calling me," many said. In addition to the call to adventure and beauty, most of us felt called to stretch our own spirits and encounter the Holy. Like those who embark on any kind of soul quest, we were called to consider how we could grow spiritually from our experience. Thus at the end of the journey our questions were "What did the mountains teach me? Why was I called to be here? How will home be different after I return? How will I be different after I return?"

Pilgrimage takes us into what I call "homescapes," places where we feel an inner rootedness, where we know intuitively that even if we are in a strange, wild, and faraway place, we are home.

Maybe you have been to a retreat or workshop that had a transforming impact on your life. You learned to meditate, perhaps, and you resolved to continue this prayerful, centering practice after you got home. And you did meditate daily, for about a month or so, before the baby was born or Dad got sick or you were promoted at work. Gradually, you slipped back into the old patterns. Then you signed up for another workshop, hoping to get a shot of spiritual inspiration that would have a more lasting effect. Your motivation for change was easier to maintain in the environment of the quest or the retreat than in the setting where you live, day to day.

For many people, what happens in the wilderness of a pilgrim journey may be similar to what happens after a retreat or workshop, but a pilgrimage transformation is more than inspiration for change. It is not necessarily even voluntary, and it is irreversible. You cannot will yourself to be transformed by the Spirit. In fact, you may not even want to change in the ways that you do as a result of your pilgrimage. You are grasped by the Holy, however, and as a result of your epiphany and your struggle, you will not relate to your world or those in it as you did before.

The pilgrim returns from homescape to home, from sacred time to clock time, from sacred space to people space. Sometimes the epiphanies of the soul that have transformed people are at odds with the lives they lived before they went on pilgrimage. As we saw in Chapter Five, Malcolm X, leader of the Black Muslim fight for racial justice, returned from the Islamic pilgrimage of the *hajj* with his heart more open to hope for human community and racial

harmony. But his new agenda threatened others in his organization, and they murdered him.

Most of us do not have to deal with such dramatic clashes. If you have felt the power of a peak experience, however, and you return home transformed, it will probably mean coming up against aspects of your life that call for, and resist, change. Your task is to bring your experience of sacred space into profane space. You cannot sustain the extraordinary experiences of religious ecstasy or *communitas,* but you want to integrate your new ways of being or thinking into your life as you move into the final stage of pilgrimage, *reincorporation.*

One of the epiphanies of my Himalayan adventure occurred at a most unlikely place and time. It was on the morning of the fourth day of the trek. The day before, during which we ascended about four thousand feet, had been particularly strenuous. We camped that night in the village of Ghorepani, where rain drizzled into fog and temperatures hovered near freezing. We huddled around the stove in a lodge for warmth as we conducted our evening check-in and had dinner. Then it was back to the tents, where I slipped into my sleeping bag wearing long underwear and kept my hat pulled over my ears. By morning, the rain had layered the ground with a crust of mud crystals, and I awoke to the sound of the voice of Pemba, the Sherpa who had brought me morning tea. Even the prospect of hot tea could not lure me from my down cocoon, but the day called me forth, and I reached over to unzip the door to the tent. Through a small opening I saw only Pemba's feet—bare, and shod merely in flip-flops. The image is permanently etched in my memory.

Pemba was not the only one without shoes. That evening I went to Lakpa, our head Sherpa, with the extra pair of shoes that I had been advised to bring along and asked him to give them to someone who could fit into them.

A few days later, I noted that my shoes were on Pemba's feet. Also, Pemba had apparently been assigned to watch out for me. Despite some trouble with my bad foot, I was quite capable of keeping up, but there he was anyway, a constant companion for the last three days of the trek.

I cannot tell you a lot about Pemba because he did not speak English. But for three days, we walked together. I have a picture of Pemba and me. I am wearing a parka that had belonged to my mother. It was an old L. L. Bean jacket she had owned for years before she died in 1983—bright red with a fur-lined hood. I have always loved the parka, and I got good use of it on the trek when we were above ten thousand feet in the snow and cold. So in the photo, there I am in my red parka, with fleece over my ears and around my neck, long underwear, and L. L. Bean's best hiking boots with thermal socks. Pemba, a young man of about twenty, is wearing a baseball cap, a worn scarf, a knit shirt, a flimsy pink and purple windbreaker—and my shoes.

During my three days with Pemba, I saw myself through his eyes. Of course, who knows what he was thinking, really. But I saw myself as a very wealthy person. The clothing I wore—not including the priceless parka—cost more than Pemba makes in several years. Even though we did not speak each other's language, we communicated, and he smiled more and more each day—a very beautiful and heartwarming smile.

At the end of the trek, as our pilgrim group packed our duffel bags, many of us left clothing there—dirty, of course—for the guides and porters. For the most part, they were items we had brought with the intention of leaving them—things we didn't want anyway. I was conscious of our being the wealthy westerners who had so much that we would not miss these various belongings.

I decided I wanted to give Pemba my mother's red parka, and I also bought a colorful new scarf for him. (He was a small man, and most of his clothing was not only trekker discards but styled for women. I wanted to give him something that was purchased just for him.) As we said good-bye, I took the scarf and put it around his neck and handed him the parka. He smiled but otherwise showed no response. I did not know what he thought. I did not know how he felt. And that was quite all right. In fact, it was a good spiritual exercise for me to give something to someone with such pleasure and get no response.

It was an incredible joy to give Pemba, not a castoff, but my precious parka, to which I had become quite attached on the trek. In a way, it was the culmination of my pilgrim journey. I did not give because of my guilt or his need but because it was what I wanted to do. I do not know if he wears it or has sold it. It does not matter.

One of the first things I did after returning from my pilgrimage to Nepal was clean out my closets and make generous donations to the church rummage sale and the shelters for homeless families and battered women. Because of my encounter with the Holy on the paths of Nepal, I was more aware of my own wealth and wastefulness. I have never been a big shopper, but I find that now I shop even less. The year following the trip, my husband, Chuck, and I prepared to move, and we downsized our household rather drastically in order to squeeze into a small house. Instead of feeling like a sacrifice, this exercise of *involuntary* simplicity felt liberating.

The practice of conscious eating (described in Chapter Four) was another aspect of pilgrimage that changed how I approached my consumer habits at home. In Nepal, where people lived so close to the land—where we saw our chicken dinner feathered and fluttering before we savored it fried and flavorful—I became more aware not just of my appreciation for what I eat but also of my participation in nature's food chain. Although I have always felt a deep connection with the wild creatures in nature, I have

conveniently managed to separate my affection for the fish and fowl of the wild from my fondness for their body parts sliced into filets. My experience on the pilgrimage sharpened my consciousness of relationship with what I eat. As a result, I decided upon returning home that I wanted to learn to fish. I thought that if I could catch something that I eat, I would feel less detached from the reality of killing the creatures that are part of my diet.

Chuck and I planned a camping trip to the Sierra Nevada, a range of mountains in central California. We set up camp next to a young couple who had been having rainbow trout every evening for dinner, so abundant were the fish in the river that flowed through the campground.

I set out to catch my first fish. Children can do this, I thought. In the clear water, I watched the trout linger near my bait. No bites. When I returned to our campsite without any fish, the young man camping next to us said he and his wife were getting tired of eating fish for dinner. He handed me several trout, cleaned and ready to cook. I asked him what kind of bait he was using, and he reached into his tackle box and gave me a spinner.

The next day I tied the magic spinner onto my line. Within a few minutes, however, the spinner was lodged in a tree root under the water. A few hours later, having polluted the river with a variety of lures, I returned to camp, where the neighbor handed me another bag of cleaned trout from his day's take.

I tried fishing again when Chuck and I went to Alaska several months later. This time it was "combat fishing" on the Kenai peninsula, where there were so many red (sockeye) salmon running, you just had to throw a hook out and wait for one to snag it. After several hours in the combat zone (trying not to snag one of my fellow anglers), I gave up, sore from the physical rigors of repeated casting and quite discouraged that I had not caught our dinner. That evening, however, we received a visit from one of the neighboring campers, with a large slab of sockeye salmon filleted and ready for the grill.

I concluded from these experiences that I had been successful at fishing, albeit in a rather unconventional way. But I had not yet had to remove a fish from my hook and take its life.

A few months later, we arrived in North Carolina, where there is a small pond on the family property, stocked with bass and bluegill. This, I decided, would be an opportunity to catch our dinner. For months, however, I avoided fishing. Perhaps I feared I would succeed. Finally, I gave it a try.

I enjoyed the experience of quiet engagement at the pond, where the rhythmic cast, plop, and reel motions were a meditation. Swallows dipped to the surface of the pond for their evening meal, and fish occasionally rippled the glassy water as they snapped up an insect appetizer, but I did not attract so much as a nibble to my line.

The next week, a neighbor brought his grandchildren to fish in the pond. "If we catch any bass, do you want some?" he asked. "Sure," I said. I was getting good at my unconventional method of catching fish, and thought I might land yet another batch cleaned and ready for the cooking pan. "Please remember to use barbless hooks," I said, wanting to reinforce compassion for the living creatures that would be the involuntary adversaries of my neighbors' afternoon sport.

The fish, three bass about a foot long, were not cleaned. They were not even dead. Two young boys presented them to me, still wiggling and flopping about.

I wanted to say, "No, put them back," but it was too late to change my mind. Chuck retreated to his study. "You're the one who wanted them," he said.

My book on the basics of fishing was packed in the camping equipment and not accessible. I tried to remember how to clean a fish. First, however, I had to kill them. I told the fish I was sorry for their suffering and for this ignoble end to their lives. It was a prayerful apology, not just to these fish, but also to all living things that die in order that I may nourish my body. Then I struck them on the head with a mallet. I had seen people do this in Alaska: How was it that it did not seem so much like murder then? As I sliced the bellies of the fish and cut off their heads, blood splattered onto my shirt and vital organs oozed out onto the newspaper. I was already covered with scales. I wanted to quit, but how could I kill three fish and then discard them? My conscience would not allow it; it would be too great a dishonor to the fish. Their bodies kept twitching, and I tried to convince myself that they were not still feeling the violence of their slaughter. I apologized to the first fish as I mutilated its flesh in an attempt to fillet it.

When I finally finished cleaning all three of the bass, I felt absurd and alone. I wrapped the heads and guts in newspaper and ceremoniously buried them deep in the compost pile, then I cried while I scrubbed my hands and arms in the kitchen sink. Like Lady Macbeth when she wrung her hands and commanded the stain of King Duncan's blood out of her heart, I knew that what had disturbed me most would not be eliminated with soap and water. But I also felt oddly proud that I had faced the task; the irremovable stain was a bond with nature, not a rift, and it would give me compassion.

Although I had lost my appetite by this time, I searched through cookbooks and found a Provençal recipe. Chopping tomatoes and parsley from the garden and pressing fresh garlic into the mixture, I began to get my appetite back. We lit new candles at the table, and I offered yet another prayer, this time in gratitude for my meal as well as for the gifts of creation. Unfortunately, even a gourmet presentation and candlelight setting could not disguise the disappointing fact that these fish, it turned out, had very little

taste. A few days later, I related my fishing saga to a neighbor, who missed the point of it altogether and quipped, "Oh, I coulda told you those lake bass aren't worth eatin'."

Although it is with some wistfulness that I recall my bungled attempts to fish and eat my catch, the outcome of all this has been that I relate more intimately to the source of my food. I do not know whether or not I will ever attempt to catch and kill my dinner again, but the prayerful and tearful experience of killing the bass and then preparing it and eating it has made me ever mindful of what it means to bite into the flesh of a creature that lived and breathed in this world.

The permanent influences of the Nepal trek on my consumer habits and my awareness of what I eat were two powerful changes for me. Others in our pilgrim band met the Holy in other ways. One man in our group, Matthew, was so dramatically affected by his journey that he was not able to return to home as he had known it.

Matthew signed on for the pilgrimage to Thailand and Nepal because he wanted to trek "the mighty Himalayas." Athletic and strong, he was usually way out ahead of the rest of us on the trail, except when he was helping others up or down a steep incline. From time to time, he would stop and play a drum, the rhythms echoing into the mountains with uplifting energy. Eager to learn about the culture and religion of the people of Asia, he engaged himself enthusiastically, though he struggled at times with the strangeness of Hindu and Buddhist images or rituals. So upbeat did he appear that it was a surprise to many of us when Matthew broke into tears one evening and told us of the pain he had been carrying for most of the week on the trail. There in the mountains—on the other side of the world from his home, his wife, and his two teenage sons—he was thinking about leaving home, permanently. For twenty-one years he had shared his life and home with Cindy, whom he had never really loved, at least not with the deep passion of a lifelong love. Now he had decided he could not stay in his marriage. Later he wrote:

> For nearly all of my 21 years of marriage, I'd wished I could have married a woman I loved. But this pilgrimage could not be a time to think about that. This was an opportunity to escape and leave behind my personal life for a while.
>
> The daily stimulation of the trip—from experiencing Buddhist temples and a primitive Thai hill country village to seeing Mount Everest by plane and hiking between 8,000-meter peaks—kept my mind off home and family until we left the remote Nepali town of Tatopani in the rain on our 15th day. I was walking at the rear, stooped

under a rain poncho. The raindrops hid my tears as I grieved the love that I never had.

Matthew perceived the group to be unreceptive to the deeper matters of the heart, particularly the kind of anguish that he suffered. Feeling disconnected from our check-in sessions, he carried his burden alone.

That night, he sat on a rock and prayed, but even God seemed absent. In his journal, he carried on a dialogue with the inner voice of his pilgrimage, a spiritual practice that our leaders had encouraged. "How's it going?" the voice of his pilgrimage asked.

"Enjoying all aspects of mountaineering," he wrote, "but finding group more concerned with aches and pains. Spiritual part of trek hard to find. How can I get back to hearing God speak to me through this trek?"

"Be alone and listen" was his answer.

The next afternoon, after we'd settled into our camp in Larjung, Matthew set out to find a birthday gift. Instead, he found a cave, where he poured out his despair. "Where is my God?" he cried. Feeling abandoned in that cave on the other side of the world from his home, he recalled verses from Psalm 139:

Whither shall I go from thy Spirit?
Or whither shall I flee from thy presence?

If I ascend to heaven, thou art there!
If I make my bed in Sheol, thou art there!

In the silence, God spoke. In the emptiness, God was there. "God was with me," Matthew wrote later. Feeling God's presence, he was ready to share his anguish with the group, and we were able to give him a community where he was held through this painful time. He was a very long way from home, and home was falling apart:

> As much as I wished to ignore or submerge my most pressing issue, the pilgrimage wouldn't allow it. Like lava forcing its way to the surface of a volcano, my ever-present deep marital turmoil forced its way into my pilgrimage.
>
> In this foreign place, apart and away, the decision I had to make seemed clear: End the marriage. To be honest about this death in the family was at the same time exhilarating and frightening. My soul had the prospect of life again, but I knew the tearing and shattering of lives would be horrific. Within hours of returning to my house, I informed my wife and boys with much sorrow and made plans to move out.
>
> Little did I know when I left for Asia in February that my pilgrimage would really only be beginning in March

when I returned to the U.S. I am continuing on my spiritual journey of the heart.

It is one thing to feel the personal liberation of a decision made on a mountaintop, feeling God's presence and embraced by a supportive community, and quite another to return to the valley of broken relationship, guilt, and pain.

Matthew had felt called to the mountains, where, in that wilderness away from home, he faced what he had tried to avoid and knew what it was he had to do upon his return. He had wanted to be touched by a peaceful God, who was absent. In his impulse to flee his turmoil, he was both pursued and held by a God of disturbing presence. The context of pilgrimage not only threw him into the chaos of his inner conflict but also gave him a holding environment, a community (flawed as it was) in which he could struggle honestly with his pain.

It is one thing to feel the personal liberation of a decision made on a mountaintop, feeling God's presence and embraced by a supportive community, and quite another to return to the valley of broken relationship, guilt, and pain.

Pilgrimage offers a context of community for people journeying together, but each person is also alone in the wilderness of his or her own pilgrim heart. It may be a time apart and away, but it is not an escape from the conflicts in our lives. For Laurey

Masterton, the ability to enter her own struggle fully in the context of supportive community was one of the gifts she received and brought back with her from her journey to Alaska.

Laurey signed up for the Alaska trip on an impulse. Enmeshed in a stressful conflict at work (one in which she had been betrayed by someone she trusted), she saw an ad in the *New York Times* that presented her with an opportunity to counter this dreadful situation by doing something good. Two thousand people were being asked to enroll for a bike ride from Fairbanks to Anchorage—510 miles, six days, 85 miles a day. For every mile they rode, they were to solicit contributions toward research on an AIDS vaccine. She did not own a bicycle, had not ever ridden more than 25 miles, and had never done any fundraising. As soon as she received the information, however, she signed up, purchased a bicycle, and began training. Recalling the final weeks she had spent with her dear friend Michael before he died from AIDS, and feeling drawn toward doing something positive that would lift her out of the negative mire of her personal situation, she raised over $22,000 and headed for Fairbanks, where the ride began. Admittedly, she also wanted to escape.

Although she was in good shape for peddling through the hills near her home in North Carolina in summer weather, Laurey was not prepared for the conditions she encountered in Alaska:

Day Two emerged cold and rainy. I had never ridden in cold rain, but there wasn't much choice. Two drenched young Inuit men danced and waved sage around, blessing us on our ride. No raincoats for them. I, cloaked in space-age fabric, figured I'd be OK.

The ride climbed to a 3,200-foot pass that morning, getting colder by the mile. At one point I was riding, completely alone, in a full snowstorm. A wet, icy, snowstorm. Local bus companies sent in warming vehicles, and some of my fellow riders piled in, shivering, wrapped in Mylar blankets. I kept riding.

At the end of the day, many of us had succumbed to the cold. Those of us who rode the whole way were exhausted and freezing. No heroics were involved here, except on the part of the medical volunteers who treated the hypothermic masses.

On Day Three, my heel gave way. My Achilles heel—a not-so-subtle message from the universe, I thought. Perhaps I hadn't stretched enough. Or maybe it was the cold that did me in. By mile 58, I could not pedal anymore. 29 miles to go for the day, but I was finished. This, not finishing, was not in my plans, not in my imagination. Not by a long shot. I sat on the side of the road with a stranger, crying and wondering about my heel, the ride, my abilities,

> my body, my age . . . all this as rider after rider cruised by. A medical volunteer picked me up. Iced my foot. Wiped my tears. Told me to wait and see. By tomorrow I might feel better. That seemed impossible to me.
>
> No part of me had planned for getting hurt. I was devastated. A healthy, fit, and self-sufficient person, I was not used to needing help. If things had ever been difficult before, I had always been able to carry on no matter what. Not this time.

Rest, ice, ibuprofen, and the caring ministrations of an orthopedic specialist produced amazing results, and Laurey was able to get back on her feet—and her wheels—for the next day's ride. She finished the race, tallying 434 miles of the 510 she had promised to complete.

Allowing herself to be helped by a stranger, experiencing pain, helplessness, and the prospect of failure—these were the unexpected setbacks that became the sacred core of Laurey's journey and empowered her to face the difficult situation that awaited her when she returned home. Not only had she made a significant contribution toward AIDS research, but she had also discovered her strength by encountering her weakness. Her faith in human companions, shaken by betrayal, was restored by the gifts of human care she received when she needed them. Orphaned at the age of

twelve and a survivor of uterine and ovarian cancer, Laurey was no stranger to suffering and hardship. But when she returned from this adventure, she was less inclined to feel she had to tough it out on her own. With her now she carried the image of divine compassion and faithfulness that had been conveyed to her in the faces and the hands of strangers. And because she had felt supported by this safety net of caring on her journey, she knew it would be there for her when she needed it again. There were times after she returned that she just wanted to be back in the ride, peddling up steep grades near glacial fields or gliding down past hauntingly blue-hued rivers rimmed by fireweed meadows—far, far away in mind and body from the problems at home. But she could not go back and retrieve the epiphany of that time.

The experience of pilgrimage cannot be sustained, but those who have received gifts of grace or revelation in extraordinary time and space can be sustained by the power of their experience when they return to ordinary time and space.

The experience of pilgrimage cannot be sustained, but those who have received gifts of grace or revelation in extraordinary time and space can be sustained by the power of their experience when they return to ordinary time and space.

In *Where the Heart Is,* a novel by Billie Letts, one of the characters says, "Home is the place that'll catch you when you fall. And we all fall."[2]

Indeed, we do. And when we fall, we need the spiritual safety net that will catch us. It is often our structures of home that collapse, however, forcing us to rely on the deeper sense of home that we create or carry within. Home is the people with whom we share our lives, and they die or leave or shut us out. Home is a domicile decorated with photographs, art, and furnishings that make it comfortable and safe, and it can be consumed by fire or eclipsed by a tornado or crumbled by an earthquake. Home is a place where we work or go to school and shop and volunteer, and we can lose our jobs or our health and be forced to move.

When the home of our own constructions crumbles—when we fall—that is when we most need the spirit home that will catch us. It is this aspect of home that speaks to me as I reflect on the situation that I encountered upon my return from sabbatical journeys in 1998.

When the home of our own constructions crumbles—when we fall—that is when we most need the spirit home that will catch us.

For seven years I had served a wounded but vital congregation, dealing with financial crises, staff transitions, and the challenges of offering spiritual leadership among people who had experienced a betrayal of trust on the part of their previous minister. I was nearing burnout when I left for sabbatical. Lay leadership had been empowered, intergenerational community was

flourishing, a fourteen-year trend of membership loss had been abated and reversed, and a culture of abundance and vision had replaced attitudes of scarcity and spiritual myopia. But I was tired, very tired.

The sabbatical of spiritual pilgrimages was what I needed, and I returned to work with renewed energy and enthusiasm for my ministry. I asked my governing board to engage with me in a conversation that would also give us the opportunity to recovenant for a new phase of ministry together. I was more relaxed and spiritually nourished by my sabbatical, and my sermons were better than ever. Attendance at Sunday worship services rose, and plans were in place for adding a second service. After several years of weeding, pruning, and preparing this congregational soil, I was finally looking forward to enjoying a time of seed and harvest.

There was no process of recovenanting, however, for the congregation's attention was diverted by a conflict over my authority to supervise a member of the staff with whom I had been in some tension.

The governing board upheld my authority, and the staff member resigned. A small group of people who were discontent with this situation reacted, however, by organizing an effort to recall my ministry. Although it was clear that they would not be able to gather the congregational support they needed, their effort precipitated a divisive congregational trauma. Feeling that

I could no longer be an effective minister to this congregation, I resigned.

"Home is the place that'll catch you when you fall. And we all fall." Before this abrupt and painful end to my eight-year ministry, it was inconceivable that I could "fall" in the context of my career, which had been charmed and blessed for seventeen years. The timing was particularly poor, as my husband had just resigned from his job because the stress was taking its toll on his health. When we considered the emotional trauma of staying in a town where we would be separated from our spiritual community and continually reminded of the pain of this upheaval (plus the financial reality of living in an expensive town on a reduced income), we decided to move. We also decided to downsize our household by about two-thirds. We sold our house, paid our debts, and put our possessions in storage. Instead of moving to a new home, however, we piled our dog and two cats into a small motor home and headed north, to Alaska.

If you have ever been through a transition that was precipitated by a traumatic change or loss, you may understand the need to put some distance between you and the painful reminders of your trauma. At the same time, you also need to be able to feel safe while you cry, vent, and heal. You are in liminal space, where, like the lobster that molts its shell and is vulnerable until it forms a new one, you are without your normal structures of protection.

It is also a time for potential growth as you seek to understand what this life experience will teach you. Going to Alaska was our way of getting away from the source of affliction in order to understand better how to deal with it. Several people told us that our misfortune would probably open the door to new adventures. We had to trust that they were right, even though we felt only loss at the time.

Lovingly launched by family, church, and friends, we set off into the unknown. We planned to go to North Carolina eventually, but our house there was leased for a few more months, so we were quite literally homeless—for the first time in our lives, we had no mailing address. Our little one-room house on wheels was like a cocoon, where we could *be* in the wilderness of our lives and our hearts and be nourished by the wild extravagant beauty of Alaska and Canada—by whales, bears, and eagles, by lakes mirroring snow-clad peaks and rivers roaring into generous waterfalls. Cut loose from our moorings of church, work, and community life, all space became home-space and all landscape became homescape.

One of the chants I had learned while on pilgrimage in Thailand and Nepal began, "I am moving on a journey to nowhere." That was what Chuck and I felt we were doing. It was OK to be adrift for a time, to follow the path of now. Except for a reservation on a ferry that would take us through Alaska's Inside Passage, we had no itinerary. Shattered by emotional upheaval, we knew we were not in a position to seek work or make any major decisions for our lives. We were angry and hurt, and we sought the solace of glacial valleys and flowering tundra. Not wanting to impose our grief on our friends again and again, we gave it to untamed rivers and calving glaciers. The wilderness received our rage and tamed us. For how could we be in such a place and not sing with gratitude for the dear gift of life?

While we wandered the wilderness, we knew that we would eventually land in North Carolina, where our safe harbor was our family home in the mountains. From there, we would listen for the call into our next life venture. For the time being, we were content to drop anchor in the waters of every day. The wilderness *was* home.

As each of these stories—Matthew's, Laurey's, and mine—illustrates, the power of the pilgrimage is in the gifts of holiness, grace, compassion, and community that sustain us through each day of our lives, where we all fall, and get up, and fall again. Often the return from one pilgrimage is the occasion for the beginning of another.

❧

The paradox of the pilgrim heart is that we must live on the growing edges of our fears in order to be safe and that we must become lost in strangeness to know we belong in it. To feel

accepted, we must know exile, and to live in harmony with the whole of creation and heal it, we must feel its pain and our part in wounding it. The more we encounter the otherness outside ourselves, the more familiar we become with the wilderness inside ourselves, and the more we understand our imperfect selves, the more we become our better selves. When we make friends with our bodies, we are more at home in nature, and when we make friends with death, we are more present to life.

The goal of any sacred journey, physical or metaphorical, is to feel more at home *at home.* Our task once we have returned is to imbue our everyday lives with a sense of grounding in our spiritual understandings—in those gifts of holy wisdom that have taught us how to be more at home no matter where we are.

RESOURCES FOR PILGRIM ADVENTURES AND FURTHER READING

Life Structure Resources and the Center for Pilgrimage Renewal, 5930 Moser Road, Boonsboro, MD 21713, (800) 432-2658.

Roy Oswald and Carol Rousch are outstanding spirit guides and tour leaders. They also operate Life Structure Resources, a wonderful source for pilgrim supplies, including tapes of chants that will enrich even a brief pilgrimage taken within minutes of home.

Whidbey Institute, P.O. Box 57, Clinton, WA 98236, (360) 341-1884; Fax: (360) 341-9360. Web site: www.whidbeyinstitute.org.

A journey to Whidbey Island and the institute is a pilgrimage in itself. In addition the institute offers guided pilgrimage experiences on the island of Iona, Scotland.

Grace Cathedral, 1100 California St., San Francisco, CA 94108. Web site: www.gracecathedral.org.

The cathedral has two labyrinths, indoor and outdoor. The web site contains a wealth of information about labyrinths, including a "labyrinth locator" (which contains almost 600 labyrinth sites in the

United States). The Cathedral also offers pilgrimage tours to the labyrinth at Chartres Cathedral, Chartres, France.

A wealth of information about pilgrimage sites and opportunities is available at "Places of Peace and Power, The Sacred Site Pilgrimages of Martin Gray," www.sacredsites.com.

Phil Cousineau, *The Art of Pilgrimage: The Seeker's Guide to Making Travel Sacred.* (Berkeley, Calif.: Conari Press, 1998).

Rich with examples of possible pilgrim adventures and grounded in the universal principles of world religions, this book also stirs reflections on what it means to travel with a pilgrim's intention. You are left on your own to take the themes to a deeper level, but there is plenty to get you started.

Jennifer Louden, *The Women's Retreat Book: A Guide to Restoring, Rediscovering, and Reawakening Your True Self—in a Moment, an Hour, a Day, or a Weekend* (San Francisco: HarperSanFrancisco, 1997).

This self-help guide is for women who want to taking time to restore their souls, and it offers an abundance of resources for creating a "container" of sacred time and space.

NOTES

Introduction

Epigraph: Carl Jung, from a letter to a former student on reassessing religious values outlined to Sigmund Freud a half century earlier, quoted in Gerhard Adler, ed. *Letters,* Vol. 1 Princeton, 73.

Chapter One

Epigraph: Kabir as quoted in *The Coming of the Cosmic Christ* by Matthew Fox (San Francisco: Harper & Row, 1988).

1. Judith Walker-Riggs, "A Cosmic Theology" in *What Unitarian Universalists Believe: Living Principles for a Living Faith* (Boston: Unitarian Universalist Denominational Grants Panel, 1987), p. 74.
2. Dylan Thomas, "Fern Hill," in *The Collected Poems of Dylan Thomas* (New York: New Directions Books, 1957), p. 178.
3. Ibid., p. 180.
4. Frederick Buechner, *The Sacred Journey* (San Francisco: HarperSanFrancisco, 1982), pp. 41–42.
5. Ibid., p. 46.
6. Douglas Adams, *The Restaurant at the End of the Universe* (New York: Pocket Books, 1982), pp. 72, 79; Walker-Riggs, "A Cosmic Theology," p. 73.

7. William Blake, *The Portable Blake* (New York: Viking Press, 1946), p. 250.
8. T. S. Eliot, "Choruses from the Rock," in *Selected Poems* (Orlando, Fla.: Harcourt Brace, 1934), p. 107.
9. Walker Percy, *The Message in the Bottle* (New York: Farrar, Straus & Giroux, 1975), p. 119.
10. Ibid., pp. 142–143.
11. Robert Frost, "The Death of the Hired Man" in *The Poetry of Robert Frost,* Edward Connery Lathem, ed. (Austin, Tex.: Holt, Rinehart and Winston, 1969), p. 38.

Chapter Two

1. Parker Palmer, *The Active Life: A Spirituality of Work, Creativity, and Caring* (San Francisco: HarperSanFrancisco, 1990), pp. 32–33.
2. Jon Kabat-Zinn, *Wherever You Go, There You Are: Mindfulness Meditation in Everyday Life* (New York: Hyperion, 1994).
3. David Wagoner, "Lost" in *Traveling Light: Collected and New Poems* (Urbana: University of Illinois Press, 1999), p. 10.
4. This can also be found in Sharon Parks, "Led to Places We Did Not Plan to Go . . . ," *The Cresset* (Valparaiso University), Summer 1996, p. 5.
5. Henry Miller, *The Paintings of Henry Miller: Paint as You Like and Die Happy, with Collected Essays by Henry Miller on the Art of*

Watercolor, Noel Young, ed. (San Francisco:, Chronicle Books, 1970), p. 77.

6. Carol Shields, *The Stone Diaries* (New York: Viking Press, 1993).
7. Henry David Thoreau, *Walden,* in *The Portable Thoreau,* Carol Bode, ed. (New York: Viking Press, 1964), p. 263.
8. Ibid., p. 561.
9. Ibid., p. 559.

Chapter Three

Epigraph: Henry David Thoreau as quoted in *The Coming of the Cosmic Christ* by Matthew Fox (San Francisco: Harper & Row, 1988).

1. Maurice Sendak, *Where the Wild Things Are* (New York: HarperCollins, 1963).
2. From a lecture by Vivienne Hull, Whidbey Institute, Whidbey Island, Wash. Lecture given May 6, 1998, in Iona, Scotland.
3. Jean Shinoda Bolen, *Crossing to Avalon* (San Francisco: HarperSanFrancisco, 1994), pp. 7–8.
4. The stages are described on Internet sites and attributed to Rev. Lauren Artress, author of *Walking a Sacred Path: Rediscovering the Labyrinth as a Spiritual Tool* (New York: Riverhead Books, 1995).
5. Pema Chödrön, *When Things Fall Apart: Heart Advice for Difficult Times* (Boston: Shambhala, 1997), p. 65.

6. *Oxford English Dictionary,* Vol. II, Oxford University Press Compact Edition. (Oxford: Oxford University Press, 1971), p. 858.
7. Jerry Godard, *Eros Plays: Parts and Pieces from a Left-Handed Psychology* (College Park, Md.: University Press of America, 1990), p. 28.

Chapter Four

Epigraph: Saraha, as quoted in *Chop Wood, Carry Water: A Guide to Finding Spiritual Fulfillment in Everyday Life* by Rick Fields, with Peggy Taylor, Rex Weyler, and Rick Ingrasci (Los Angeles: J. P. Tarcher, 1984).

1. Peter Fleck, *The Blessings of Imperfection* (Boston: Beacon Press, 1987), pp. 17–18.
2. Jaroslav Pelikan, "Lectures on Genesis" in *Luther's Works,* Vol. 1 (Saint Louis, Mo.: Concordia Publishing House, 1958), p. 116.
3. Carl Sandburg, "Accept Your Face with Serious Thanks" in *Breathing Tokens* (New York: Harcourt, Brace, Jovanovich, 1978), p. 154.
4. I discuss this topic in depth in *Remembering Well: Rituals for Celebrating Life and Mourning Death* (San Francisco: Jossey-Bass, 2000).
5. There are notable exceptions, particularly in the Jewish and Muslim traditions.
6. Lewis Thomas, *The Lives of a Cell: Notes of a Biology Watcher* (New York: Bantam Books, 1974), p. 116.

7. From a lecture by Vivienne Hull, Whidbey Institute, Whidbey Island, Wash. Lecture given May 6, 1998, in Iona, Scotland.
8. Quoted in Graham White, *Sacred Summits: John Muir's Greatest Climbs* (Edinburgh: Canongate Books, 1999), p. xiii.
9. Maureen Killoran, "A Touch of Celt," a sermon delivered at the Unitarian Universalist Church in Asheville, N.C., Jan. 17, 1999.

CHAPTER FIVE

Epigraph: Carter Heyward, *Our Passion for Justice: Images of Power, Sexuality, and Liberation* (New York: Pilgrim Press, 1984).

1. Victor Turner, *The Ritual Process: Structure and Antistructure* (Ithaca, N.Y.: Cornell University Press, 1969), p. vii.
2. William James, *The Varieties of Religious Experience: A Study in Human Nature* (New York: Mentor Edition—New American Library, 1958), pp. 292–294.
3. Ibid., p. 306.
4. Thomas, *The Lives of a Cell,* pp. 31–32.
5. Ibid., p. 2.
6. Lewis Thomas, *Late Night Thoughts on Listening to Mahler's Ninth Symphony* (New York: Bantam Books, 1984), pp. 101–105.
7. Edward O. Wilson, *Consilience: The Unity of Knowledge* (New York: Knopf, 1998).
8. Quoted in Victor Turner, "The Center Out There: Pilgrim's Goal," *History of Religions,* 1973, *12*(3), 193.

9. Quoted in ibid., p. 219.

CHAPTER SIX

Epigraph: Henry David Thoreau as quoted in *The Coming of the Cosmic Christ* by Matthew Fox (San Francisco: Harper & Row, 1988).

1. Tony Hiss, *The Experience of Place: A Completely New Way of Looking at and Dealing with Our Radically Changing Cities and Countryside* (New York: Knopf, 1990), p. 37.
2. Billie Letts, *Where the Heart Is* (New York: Warner Books, 1995), p. 19.

THE AUTHOR

Sarah York is a writer and minister living near Asheville, North Carolina, with her husband, Chuck Campbell. She graduated with honors from Wake Forest University (B.A.) and Duke University (M.A.T.) and taught high school English for eleven years before she trained for the ministry at Harvard Divinity School (M.Div.), where she received highest distinction as a Hopkins Shareholder. During her nineteen years as a Unitarian Universalist minister, she has served congregations in New York, Maryland, California, and England. She is author of the critically acclaimed book *Remembering Well: Rituals for Celebrating Life and Mourning Death* (Jossey-Bass, 2000).

C R E D I T S